This book is dedicated to our mothers, Agnes Antizzo and Helen Howren with whom we took our first stitch. To Jack Howren, Janet Robertson, and Joe Antizzo who encouraged us. To Anne Brown who introduced us to each other. To Sue Jennings and Ann Caswell, the best mentors anyone could ever have. To Michael Boren who encouraged us to "start writing it down." To Kaz Caswell who came up with the perfect title. To Bruce Hoskins and David and Todd Wuehrmann for living with us and providing support while we wrote.

We also want to express our thanks to Janet Robertson, Anne Brown, Ann Caswell, Michael Boren and Patricia Worrel for all their proof reading and editing help. We wouldn't have been able to do it without you!

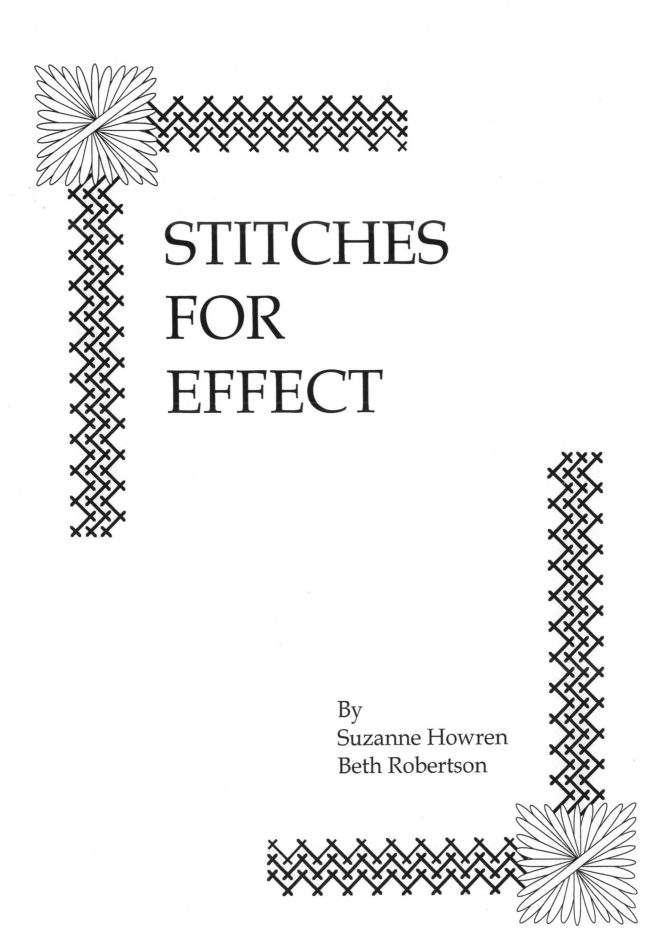

STITCHES
FOR
EFFECT

By
Suzanne Howren
Beth Robertson

TABLE OF CONTENTS

INTRODUCTION

When an artist paints a canvas or charts a design, the groundwork is laid for a stitcher's interpretation of the design. There are many painted canvases and charted designs available today that in themselves are beautiful works of art. When we first began to stitch, we believed that one could take any thread, stitch a painted canvas or charted design and have a great piece of needlework. What we have since discovered is that to achieve an effect, you must understand the properties of the thread, what it is made of, how it is dyed and how best to show off its attributes.

With the information provided in this book, you should be able to transform your canvases or designs into something closer to what the artist envisioned. You can make areas painted or charted like snow glisten as if the snow had just fallen. You can make ribbons and bows look like satin and Santa's beard feel soft and fuzzy! You can also add texture and depth.

Historical research shows the earliest examples of decorative stitch usage to be in samplers. In these antique samplers, some dating back as far as the 17th Century, you will find many different stitches. In a 17th Century English sampler in the Goodhart Collection you will find many decorative stitches including Florentine, Hungarian, Cross and Eyelet. These same stitches are still used in needlework today. If your preference is to stitch on fabric, use this book to experiment with different threads and stitches, and to expand your stitch repertoire.

With the right thread and the right stitch you can bring a design into the next dimension!

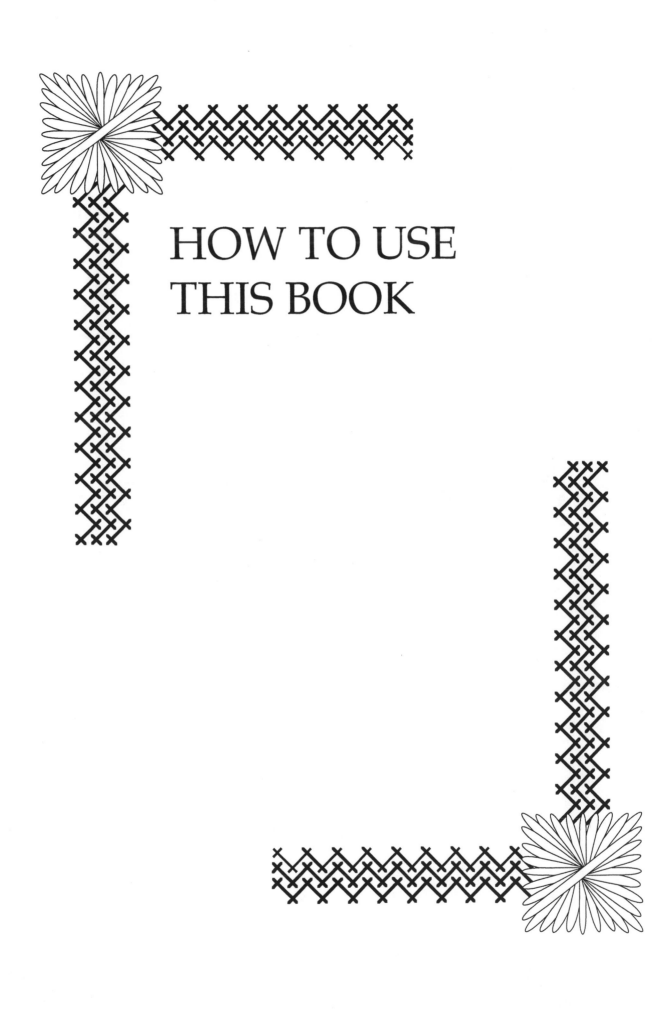

HOW TO USE
THIS BOOK

HOW TO USE THIS BOOK

Our goal in writing this book is to provide you, the stitcher, with a new tool for effectively using decorative stitches with many of the wonderful threads available today. We hope this book is useful for embellishing canvas and creating original designs; but most of all, we hope that we change the way you look at stitching, whether it be needlepoint, surface stitching or cross stitching.

There are many stitches for canvas work and we have focused on 100 of our favorites. We offer you suggestions on how to use these stitches to create various effects on your chosen ground, whether it be canvas or fabric. We also make thread suggestions—threads that we have found to be particularly effective for particular looks—that's why we have titled this book *Stitches for Effect*.

We would like you to first think about how you want an area to look—do you want it shiny, matte or textured? Then, think about whether you want to emphasize the stitch or the thread or the color. These considerations help you choose the right thread and the right stitch to create the effect you want.

TERMINOLOGY

To help you use this book efficiently, we need to clarify a few basic terms. First of all, we refer to *threads*, those materials you use to embellish fabric and canvas, which come in several different types. Thread types mentioned in this book are cotton, linen, metallic, rayon, silk, synthetic, and wool.

We also need to distinguish between the terms strand and ply. Stranded cotton is referred to as embroidery cotton and cotton floss. This thread is six-stranded and is easily divisible into 6 separate units. These units are commonly referred to as *plies*. Consequently, for the purposes of discussion in this book, we will use the term plies to refer to separate units of a thread. For example, if we suggest 2 plies of stranded cotton the reader will understand that we are referring to 2 units from that strand. In the case of pearl cotton, which is generally thought of as a soft twisted single strand thread, the reader will understand we are using the term *strand* as a single unit of thread. In the chart on page 17, which recommends thread usage on ground fabric, a number followed by the letter *P* refers to the number of plies. All other numbers refer to strands.

The terms stranded cotton and stranded silk are used throughout this book.

There are many multi-colored threads available that are referred to as *overdyed*. Some of these threads actually are overdyed, which according

to Lois Caron of the Caron Collection is defined as "dyeing one color on top of, or over, a previously dyed color." Another technique used to create many of the multi-colored threads, is *space-dying*. According to Elaine Warner of Needle Necessities, space-dyed means that the dye is "sprinkled, brushed, dipped or air-brushed on to the thread. Spacing of color is somewhat even and the majority of the time space-dyed threads have varied coloration." Watercolours and Madras are perfect examples of space-dyed threads. Since both methods create a multi-colored product, we use overdyed in our stitching suggestions to refer to both thread types.

Ground fabric is the medium you have chosen for your work. Mono canvas for the use of decorative stitching is usually more effective and easier to work on than interlock canvas. Mono canvas is available in several different mesh sizes, corresponding to the number of canvas threads in each inch of the canvas: 10 mesh canvas has 10 threads per inch, 12 mesh has 12 threads, 13 mesh has 13 threads, 14 mesh has 14 threads, and 18 mesh has 18 threads. Canvas is also available in several different colors, particularly 18 mesh. However, white and brown are the most common.

Congress Cloth is 22, 23 or 24 threads-per-inch, depending on the manufacturer, and looks and feels like mono canvas. Linen canvas is also available and works very well for decorative stitching.

Fabric is another possibility for use as a stitching ground; this includes cotton fabrics such as Aida, blends such as Lugana and Jobelan, and linen. We do recommend the use of a frame or stretcher bars when doing decorative stitches on canvas or fabric.

As stitchers, our preference is to use 18 mesh mono canvas. Many of our suggestions in this book refer to the use of threads on 18 mesh canvas. If your preference is a larger or smaller count canvas or fabric, refer to the Thread-Canvas/Fabric Conversion Chart or page 17 to obtain the corresponding ply or strand count for proper coverage.

There are diagrams for each of the stitches described in this book. Each stitch is drawn on a grid and each line in the grid represents 1 canvas or fabric thread. The individual stitches in each graph are numbered. When stitching, your needle will come up at odd numbers and go down at even numbers. Start each stitch at number *1* and follow the numbers through the stitching sequence. Some stitches have multiple paths. For these stitches the second pass will begin with a lower case *a*. The third sequence will start with an upper case *A*.

Darning patterns are stitched in the running stitch in which your thread is drawn over and under the threads of your canvas or fabric. Each row must be stitched completely from one side to the other and then back again.

TECHNIQUES

Two useful and necessary techniques for effective stitching are the stripping and laying of threads. *Stripping* means separating the plies or strands of the thread and then putting them back together. This makes the threads look smoother and spread more easily. *Laying threads* refers to the technique of using a laying tool (or a large needle, a collar stay, or your finger) to keep multiple strands or plies side by side while stitching on your canvas or fabric. This keeps the threads from looking twisted and allows them to spread to cover the area well. Some threads require careful laying on both the front and back of your work in order to create the most pleasing effect.

FEATURES

The second section of this book, "Thread Descriptions," contains descriptions of all the threads mentioned throughout the book. This information was gathered from thread manufacturers and distributors and we are passing their descriptions on to you. This section also contains two charts. The "Thread to Canvas/Fabric Conversion Chart" lists suggested threads alphabetically with canvas and fabric size recommendations. Here you can find the recommended number of strands or plies of each thread for use on the size canvas or fabric you have chosen. The "Manufacturers and Distributors Chart" lists the thread and its manufacturer or distributor. And, at last, the stitches! In the third section, "Stitches and Effects," the stitches are listed alphabetically. For each stitch, suggestions for creating effects as well as several thread choices are presented. In addition, a numbered diagram for creating each stitch is included. A grid page is also included for you to experiment with your own stitches. Finally, the "Bibliography" lists all the sources we consulted in our attempts to diagram and properly name, as well as cross reference, the stitches.

There are four indexes in the book. The first is the "Thread Index." This refers you to stitches we recommend for use with each of the threads mentioned in the book. The second, the "Stitch Index", refers you to the exact page the stitch you need is on. This index is cross-referenced with as many different names for each stitch as we were able to find. The third index is the "Effect Index." Here you can find subjects or names of items you may want to stitch. For instance: trees, Santa's coat, roads, and hair are just a few of the many effects you can look up. Each topic lists the pages on which you can find a stitch to create the effect you want to achieve. The fourth index is a "General Index" which includes listings of general topics included in the book.

We certainly hope you find this book helpful and easy to use. We had great fun researching and writing it. Happy Stitching!!!

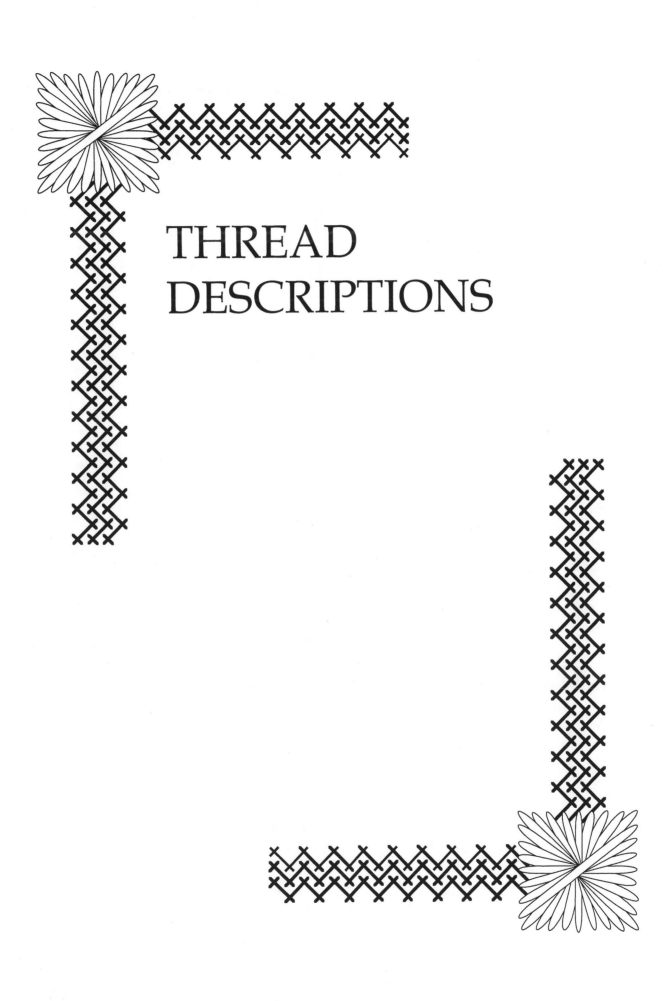

THREAD DESCRIPTIONS

THREAD DESCRIPTIONS

COTTON

Bravo! (Rainbow Gallery) A fine, 4-strand, overdyed, pliable 100% cotton thread made in the USA. It is equivalent to #12 pearl cotton when stripped. When using multiple plies, strip them and put them back together before stitching. Bravo! is dyed to match Overture and Encore! It is packaged in 15 yd. cards and is available in 33 colors.

Cotton Embroidery Floss (Anchor, DMC) A 6-strand, 100% cotton thread commonly referred to as stranded cotton. It is one of the most versatile threads available. This thread should be stripped before using to obtain a smoother effect and better coverage. It is packaged in 8.7 yd. skeins. The Anchor color range consists of 422 solid colors and 22 variegated colors. The DMC color range has 394 solid colors and 36 variegated colors.

Encore! (Rainbow Gallery) A 4-ply, overdyed, 100% cotton thread. One ply is equivalent to #8 pearl cotton. It is made in the USA, packaged in 10 yd. cards, and available in 56 colors dyed to match Overture and Bravo!.

Floche (Julia Golson Designs) A single strand cotton thread manufactured by DMC and imported from Europe by Julia Golson Designs. This thread does not need to be stripped. Use about half of the amount you would use of stranded cotton. If you normally use 6 plies of stranded cotton, use 3 strands of Floche. This thread is very easy to control and can be used for the same forms of needlework for which you would use stranded cotton. This thread is available in 85 colors which match DMC color numbers. It is sold in 40 yd. packages or 150 yd. skeins.

Floss Overdyed (Needle Necessities, Inc.) A 100% Egyptian cotton, overdyed by hand resulting in a subtle, shaded effect. These are overdyed threads generally of the same color family. Use the thread color as it comes from the skein to obtain a striped effect. Combine Floss Overdyed with a complementary solid color for a tweeded effect. To obtain a mottled effect, reverse some of the plies. This thread is packaged in 20 yd. skeins and is available in 90 colors.

Flower Thread (DMC Corporation) A twisted, cotton thread with a flat finish. The twist makes this thread difficult to lay flat when using multiple strands and long stitches. It works well for basketweave and darning patterns. It is available in 180 colors.

Madras (Needle Necessities, Inc.) An 8-ply, 100% cotton thread. This "denimized" thread is space-dyed in a unique process which creates an

old, worn look similar to stone-washed denim. Madras can be used on all sizes of ground fabric. The manufacturer suggests combining several plies of Madras with one strand of pearl cotton, letting the threads twist around each other for an intriguing effect. Madras is available in 18 colors and packaged in 10 yd. skeins.

Matte 18 (Rainbow Gallery) A single strand, matte cotton thread that fits on 18 mesh canvas. This thread is equivalent to #5 pearl cotton and is made in Belgium and Brazil. It is packaged in 15 yd. cards and is available in 55 colors. Use short threads when stitching.

Matte Cotton (DMC) A single strand, cotton thread that fits on 12, 13, and 14 mesh canvas. This thread is equivalent to #3 pearl cotton. It is packaged in 11 yd. skeins and is available in 213 colors. This thread works best when used for diagonal stitches.

Overture (Rainbow Gallery) A 4-ply, overdyed cotton in which one ply is equivalent to #5 pearl cotton. It is available in 93 colors and is dyed to match Encore! and Bravo!. Overture is packaged in 10 yd. cards.

Pearl 8 Overdyed (Needle Necessities Inc.) A 100% twisted cotton that is overdyed by hand. These are overdyed threads generally of the same color family. It is packaged in 20 yd. skeins and is available in 33 colors, compatible with Floss Overdyed colors.

Pearl Cotton (Anchor, DMC Corporation) A softly twisted, 100% cotton thread that is available in 4 sizes. The number assigned to the thread indicates the size: the smaller the number, the thicker the thread. Choose the appropriate size for your fabric or canvas ground and use this thread as it comes off the skein or ball.

Anchor packages these threads in the following colors and sizes:

#3	15 yd. skeins,	173 solid colors
#5	23 yd. skeins,	264 solid colors, 22 variegated colors
#8	85 yd. balls,	188 solid colors, 22 variegated colors
#12	58 yd. balls	36 solid colors

DMC packages these threads in the following colors and sizes:

#3	16.4 yd. skeins,	181 solid colors
#5	27.3 yd. skeins,	286 solid colors, 20 variegated colors
	53 yd. balls	114 solid colors
#8	95 yd. balls,	201 solid colors, 31 variegated colors
#12	141 yd. balls	39 solid colors

Pebbly Perle (Rainbow Gallery) A 4-ply, 100% mercerized cotton that has a cable appearance. It may be used as it comes off the card or stripped. It is made in England and France and is available in 74 colors in 10 yd. cards.

Spring II (Needle Necessities, Inc.) A 50% cotton and 50% rayon thread which creates a combination effect, matte and sheen. This thread is billed as a non-divisible thread; however, the manufacturer suggests dividing the thread for an interesting effect. Spring II is packaged in 20 yd. skeins and is available in 60 colors.

Spring II Shadowdyed (Needle Necessities, Inc.) A hand-dyed, tone-on-tone coloration of Spring II. It is packaged in 20 yd. skeins and is available in 18 colors.

Watercolours (the Caron Collection) A 3-ply, hand-dyed pima cotton in variegated colors. It has a silky sheen, especially when used in long, flat stitches. Separate the plies and use one or more as required by the ground fabric. One ply is about the same weight as a #5 pearl cotton or 6 plies of stranded cotton or 1 ply of Persian wool. This thread is packaged in 10, 40, and 100 yd. skeins and is available in 121 colors that coordinate with Wildflowers.

Wildflowers (the Caron Collection) A single strand, hand-dyed cotton in variegated colors. It has a matte finish when stitched. Use one or more strands as required by the ground fabric or canvas. One strand is approximately the same weight as flower thread or Medici Wool. It is between a #8 and #12 pearl cotton. It is available in all the same colors as Watercolours and the two threads can be used very successfully together for hardanger embroidery. It is available in 36, 120, and 400 yd. skeins.

LINEN

Backgrounds Natural Flax (Rainbow Gallery) A 100% linen thread that is undyed and made in Switzerland for use on 12 to 14 mesh canvas. It is available in the natural color only and packaged in 20 yd. cards.

Backgrounds Natural Linen (Rainbow Gallery) A 100% undyed linen thread for use on 18 mesh canvas, made in Switzerland and available on 30 yd. cards in the natural color only. This thread tends to untwist and knot easily. When stitching, give your thread a counter twist.

Rainbow Linen (Rainbow Gallery) A 100% linen made in Sweden. Some of the colors are coordinated to match 18 mesh canvas and 25-28 count evenweave linen. This makes it an excellent choice for pulled thread, darning stitches and other open stitches. It is available in 70 colors and packaged in 20 yd. cards.

METALLIC

Antica (the Caron Collection) A heavier metallic in antique shades. The effect is more of a soft glow than a shiny sparkle. It ravels easily, but can be controlled by a dab of Fraycheck or clear nail polish at one end. Before threading the needle, snap the length of thread gently to tighten the chainette and make the stitching easier. It is a little bit thicker than #5 pearl cotton, but not as thick as #3 pearl cotton. Use on 18 or 14 mesh canvas. It is fine for bargello stitches on 22/24 count Congress Cloth. Antica is available in 10 colors and is packaged in 10 yd. skeins.

Candlelight (the Caron Collection) This soft, fine metallic from the YLI Corporation is distributed by the Caron Collection. It is very flexible and although it frays, it does not break down during stitching, making it easy to handle. In weight it is very similar to Wildflowers. Use one or more strands as required by the ground fabric. Candlelight has excellent light reflective qualities; but for this reason, the structure of more complex stitches is often obscured. It is available in 20 colors on 75 yd. spools and 10 yd. cards.

Cresta d'Oro (Rainbow Gallery) A metallized polyester and rayon chainette thread made in Italy and England. This thread is packaged in 15 yd. cards and is available in 29 colors.

Fyre Werks (Rainbow Gallery) A shiny metallic ribbon made in Germany that is 55% polyester and 45% nylon. Use short stitching lengths to avoid fraying. Be sure to lay your threads flat and avoid twisting. Fyre Werks is packaged in 10 yd. cards and is available in 15 colors.

Gold Rush 14 (Rainbow Gallery) Formerly called Goldfingering, this chainette metallic thread, made in England, is 20% metallized polyester and 80% viscose. It is packaged in 10 yd. cards and is available in 58 solid colors and 19 variegated colors.

Gold Rush 18 (Rainbow Gallery) Formerly called Gold Dust, this chainette metallic is 33% metallized polyester and 67% viscose. Also made in England, this thread is available in 27 colors and packaged in 10 yd. cards and 110 yd. spools.

Kreinik Very Fine (#4) Braid (Kreinik Mfg. Co.) A relatively new, very fine metallic braid. While this thread is fine and soft, it is still very strong. It fits nicely on 22/24 count canvas and is excellent for all sizes of fabrics. It is available in 24 colors and packaged on 12 yd. reels.

Kreinik Fine (#8) Braid (Kreinik Mfg. Co.) A metallic braid that works well on 22/24 mesh canvas and is available in 138 colors on 11 yd. reels. On 18 mesh canvas, combine this thread with 3 plies of a coordinating color of stranded cotton for a subtle shimmering effect.

Kreinik Medium (#16) Braid (Kreinik Mfg. Co.) A metallic braid that works well on 18 mesh canvas for both straight and diagonal stitches. It also provides good coverage for basketweave on 14 mesh canvas. This thread can also be couched on 18 or 22/24 mesh canvas. It comes in 138 colors and is packaged on 11 yd. reels.

Kreinik Heavy (#32) Braid (Kreinik Mfg. Co.) A metallic braid that works best on large count canvas such as 13 or 14. It can also be couched on smaller count canvas. This thread comes in 5.5 and 11 yd. reels and is available on 114 colors.

Kreinik 1/8" Ribbon (Kreinik Mfg. Co.) A wonderful flat metallic 1/8 inch-wide ribbon that is perfect for 12 to 14 mesh canvas. It provides excellent coverage for diagonal stitches and also works well for long stitches. Lay this thread to prevent twisting. It is available in 128 colors and packaged on 5.5 and 11 yd. reels.

Kreinik 1/16" Ribbon (Kreinik Mfg. Co.) A flat metallic 1/16 inch-wide ribbon that is perfect for 18 mesh canvas and is available in 128 colors. It provides nice coverage for long stitches as well as diagonal stitches. This thread should be laid to prevent twisting. It is packaged on 5.5 and 11 yd. reels.

Kreinik Cord (Kreinik Mfg. Co.) A 3-ply, twisted cord that can be used for darning patterns and open canvas work on smaller count canvas and fabric. Multiple strands may also be used for small stitch areas. Its colors coordinate with Kreinik's line of braids and it is an excellent choice for couching. It is available in 24 colors on 55 yd. reels.

Kreinik Ombre (Kreinik Mfg. Co.) An 8-ply, softly twisted metallic. It can be used as is or stripped. Ombre is available on 16.5 yd. reels in solid gold, silver, pearl and 9 variegated colors.

Lacquered Jewels (Sarah Bennett Specialties) This lovely and soft metallic from the Madeira company is packaged by Sarah Bennett. The combination of 20% polyester (providing the metallic look) and 80% black rayon provides elegant sheen and sparkle, as well as strength. Use long stitches to obtain the best results. It is available in 19 colors in 50 yd. skeins.

Metallic Ribbon Floss (Designing Women, Unltd.) A 1/16 inch braided metallic and nylon ribbon. This thread spreads out on larger canvas sizes and compresses for smaller canvas sizes. It is available in 16 colors on 30 yd. spools (Opal is only available on 20 yd. spools).

Pizzaz (Renaissance Designs) A soft, metallic thread with lots of sparkle. It is available in 29 colors, 4 of which are variegated, and packaged in 10 yd. skeins.

Reflection Collection (Designing Women, Unltd.) A metallic braid that works well for needlepoint or counted thread. It is available in 16 colors on 15 yd. spools.

Shimmer (Renaissance Designs) A twisted rayon spun with pearl Pizzaz with a different effect and color range from Sprinkles. It is available in 15 colors that coordinate with Moon Glow and is packaged in 10 yd. skeins.

Sprinkles (Renaissance Designs) This thread is a 5-ply, spun polyester fiber that is combined with 6-ply Pearl Pizzaz. It has a gentle sparkle and gives the same effect as combining threads with blending filament. It is available in 41 colors that coordinate with Pure & Simple and is packaged in 10 yd. skeins.

Super Twist (Sarah Bennett Specialties) This fine gauge, sparkly metallic is from the Madeira company. It can be used alone or combined with other threads. It is available in 42 colors in 100 yd. skeins.

Tiara (Rainbow Gallery) This is a twisted, French metallic thread that is 65% viscose and 35% polyester. Use short lengths when stitching to avoid fraying. Tiara is packaged in 10 yd. cards and 31 colors.

Ultra Sprinkles (Renaissance Designs) This thread is a 5-ply spun polyester that is spun with 6-ply Pizzaz in a matching color. It sparkles gently and is like using blending filament without the fuss. It comes in 10 colors and is packaged in 10 yd. skeins.

RAYON

Fiesta! (Rainbow Gallery) A 6-ply, 100% shiny rayon that is packaged in 12 yd. cards and available in 50 colors, 8 of which are shaded colors. Separate each ply before stitching. You may stitch with plies doubled through your needle. When starting and ending threads, be sure to fasten securely.

Marlitt (Anchor) A 4-ply, shiny, 100% viscose rayon thread. After separating each ply, double the plies in your needle for better control of the thread while stitching. It is packaged in 10 yd. skeins and available in 90 colors.

Moon Glow (Renaissance Designs) A soft shiny twisted rayon. This thread is the non metallic partner of Shimmer. It is available in 15 colors that coordinate with Shimmer and is packaged in 10 yd. skeins.

Neon Rays (Rainbow Gallery) A shiny, 100% rayon ribbon made in Germany and available in 90 colors. This versatile thread spreads out on larger canvas sizes and compresses for smaller canvas sizes. To lay threads flat you must first get rid of the kinks. Dampen your working

length of thread and let dry before stitching. Neon Rays is packaged in 10 yd. cards and is available in 90 colors.

Patina (Rainbow Gallery) A twisted, shiny, 100% rayon thread that is made in the USA. This thread may be stripped. Use short stitching lengths and be sure to maintain the twist of the thread. It is packaged in 15 yd. cards and is available in 85 colors.

Rayon Ribbon Floss (Designing Women, Unltd.) A versatile, shiny, $^{1}/16$ inch braided rayon ribbon. This thread spreads out on larger canvas sizes and compresses for smaller canvas sizes. It is available in 30 colors on 40 yd. reels.

SILK

Backgrounds Helene (Rainbow Gallery) A single ply, 100% silk thread made in Switzerland. Use medium lengths to stitch. Available in white and black on 20 yd. cards.

Backgrounds Natural Silk (Rainbow Gallery) A single ply 100% Noppee silk made in Switzerland. Stitch with shorter than normal lengths to avoid fraying. Available in the natural color only on 20 yd. cards.

Backgrounds Silk & Cream (Rainbow Gallery) A single strand thread made in Switzerland that is 50% silk and 50% wool. This thread is available in 12 colors on 20 yd. cards.

Empress Silk (Needle Necessities) A recently introduced 100% pure Chinese silk. It is a 6-ply thread that has the softness of silk and the shine of rayon. It can be stripped and used on any size canvas or fabric. It comes in 8.7 yd. skeins and is available in 105 solid colors that are compatible with both Anchor and DMC and 18 overdyed colors.

Impressions (the Caron Collection) A 50% wool, 50% silk blend. It comes in solid colors that coordinate with Soie Cristale silk and hand-dyed colors that coordinate with Watercolours and Waterlilies. It is about the same weight as Wildflowers, but has more loft. It is very versatile and can be used on fine linens as well as larger counts for needlepoint canvas. You can often control the look of your stitches to create either a sculptured or satiny effect simply by adding or subtracting one strand. The blend of wool and silk produces a unique appearance as the two fibers reflect light differently, giving your stitching great depth. There are 60 solid and 38 variegated colors that are available in 36 yd., 120 yd., and 400 yd. skeins.

Kreinik Silk Mori (Kreinik Mfg. Co.) A 6-ply, spun silk that has a rich sheen. It is easily divisible and therefore works well on all sizes of canvas

and fabric. This thread is available in 5 yd. skeins in 75 colors that have been dyed to match Kreinik Silk Serica.

Kreinik Silk Serica (Kreinik Mfg. Co.) A 3-ply filament silk with a splendid sheen. It may be used as is or stripped for a soft, rippled effect. When stripping this thread, Kreinik suggests dampening the silk before stitching to relax the ripples and leave a flat area with an especially high sheen. This thread is available on 11 yd. reels in 75 colors that have been dyed to match Kreinik Silk Mori.

Silk/Wool (J. L. Walsh Company) A 50% silk and 50% wool 5-ply hand-dyed thread. This wonderfully soft thread has a nice sheen and is easy to stitch with. Some of the colors provide a mottled or tweeded effect. This thread is available in a wide assortment of colors and comes in 12 yd. skeins.

Soie Cristale (the Caron Collection) A 12-ply, solid-color, spun silk. Use the solid colors the same as you would use Waterlilies which is dyed on natural or white Soie Cristale. It has a superb range of 128 colors and is available in 6 yd. and 33 yd. skeins.

Soie d'Alger (Access Commodities, Kreinik Mfg. Co.) A 7-ply spun silk that is easily divisible and available in 416 colors. Strip this thread prior to stitching and be sure to lay the plies to obtain the luster of this silk. Kreinik packages it in 5.5, 43, and 383 yd. skeins. Access Commodities packages it in 8 and 45 meter hanks.

Splendor (Rainbow Gallery) A 12-ply, 100% silk that is made in France and available in 83 colors on 8 yd. cards. This thread should be stripped and put back together before stitching. Use a laying tool while stitching to maintain the shine of this thread.

Trebizond (Access Commodities) A twisted, long filament, silk thread. It is excellent for basketweave on 18 mesh canvas. The manufacturer suggests long stitches to showcase the luster of this long filament silk; pad the area with pearl or matte cotton first to obtain better coverage and a "puffed up" effect. The manufacturer also suggests stripping this thread for use on finer mesh canvas and fabric. Once stripped, the thread has a crinkly look. Trebizond is sold on 10 meter reels and is available in 84 colors.

Waterlilies (the Caron Collection) A 12-ply hand-dyed variegated silk. It gives a subtle sheen when stitched and has particularly good light reflection qualities. Use a single ply for very fine work or as many plies as necessary to suit your ground fabric. Many of the colors match Watercolours and Wildflowers, but because the silk fibers take the dye differently, they may be more subdued. It is available in 6, 40, and 100 yd. skeins and comes in 79 colors.

SYNTHETIC

Charleston (Needle Necessities) This fuzzy thread is 100% polyamid with a chain center and no core. It is made in Italy and is hand-dyed in the U.S. It is recommended that you stitch this thread into your piece last so that you don't catch any of the fuzzy threads. Charleston is available in 8 yd. skeins and comes in 37 hand-dyed colors.

Crystal Rays (Rainbow Gallery) This thread is a tubular, overdyed nylon netting (Rhapsody) with a metallic core made in the USA. It is packaged in 5 yd. cards and is available in 59 colors. Stitch with short lengths and pull it tight. Cut the thread on the diagonal to avoid fraying.

Double Dipped Rachel (the Caron Collection) One color of Rachel threaded through another. It is very thick and works best on counts of 14 or coarser, although it can be couched down on finer fabrics. The colors of Double Dipped Rachel, even pastels, tend to be complex and rich. There are 54 colors available in 5 yd. skeins.

Flair (Rainbow Gallery) A 100% nylon tubular thread that provides a glistening effect. It is made in England and is available in 84 colors on 10 yd. cards. Use short stitching lengths and cut ends on the diagonal to avoid fraying.

Frosty Rays (Rainbow Gallery) A tubular nylon thread with a metallic core that is a combination of Flair and Tiara. This thread is available in three varieties: Gloss Colors (colors of Flair with colors of Tiara), Pearl Colors (colors of Flair with white pearl Tiara), and Ice Colors (white Flair with colors of Tiara). These combinations provide a total of 148 available colors and are packaged in 5 yd. cards. Stitch with short lengths and pull tight. Cut the thread on the diagonal to avoid fraying.

Kit Kin (the Caron Collection) An Angora-like blend that can be used to simulate fur or hair. Its fine texture is best used in combination with another thread in the needle, such as stranded cotton, to give it bulk. Interesting shading effects can be achieved by combining it with one of the hand-dyed threads such as Watercolours, Wildflowers, Waterlilies or variegated Impressions. It is best stitched after other stitching has been completed. It can be gently brushed to give a furry appearance. Kit Kin is available in 10 yd. skeins in 11 colors.

Patent Leather (Rainbow Gallery) A 60% polyester and 40% polyurethane thread that is $^1/16$ of an inch wide and made in Japan. It is available in 4 colors on 2 yd. cards. This thread must be laid on the front and back of the canvas when using long stitches.

Per"Suede" (Renaissance Designs) A 100% rayon thread that looks and feels like Ultrasuede. It has a 50% cotton and 50% polyester backing that

adds strength to the thread and makes stitching easier. It comes in 5 yd. skeins and is available in 10 colors.

Pure & Simple (Renaissance Designs) A 10-ply polyester thread that forms the base for Sprinkles. Without the metallic, this thread provides a matte finish. It is available in 10 yd. skeins in 41 colors that coordinate with Sprinkles.

Rachel (the Caron Collection) A tubular, nylon thread. It compresses or expands to accommodate a large variety of canvas or fabric sizes. It has a shimmery, wet look and a transparent appearance when stitched flat; compressed, it is more opaque. In addition to using it for traditional stitching, other fibers can be threaded through it or it can be stitched on top of other needlework. To prevent the thread from unraveling while stitching, cut threads at an angle. Rachel is available in 10, 40, or 100 yd. skeins in 55 colors.

Rachel Overdyed (Needle Necessities) A 100% nylon thread which is machined as a flat tube. It is then overdyed by hand which produces some interesting effects. This thread comes in 10.67 yd. skeins and is available in 22 colors.

Rachelette (the Caron Collection) Rachel with a fine metallic threaded through it. The sparkle of the metallic combined with the shimmer of the Rachel can give your work a truly dazzling effect. It is usually best for counts of 14 or coarser, but long stitches will work on 18 or on 22/24 count canvas. It comes in 5 yd. skeins and is available in 63 colors.

Rhapsody (Rainbow Gallery) A 100% nylon, tubular, overdyed ribbon made in the USA. It is packaged in 8 yd. cards and is available in 42 overdyed colors, including 14 that are monochromatic. Stitch with short lengths and pull it tight. Cut the thread on the diagonal to avoid fraying.

Snow (the Caron Collection) An opalescent, synthetic thread. It is very easy to work with and in weight is similar to #5 pearl cotton, 6 plies of stranded cotton, or 1 ply of Persian wool. It tends to pick up the colors used around it. Although it has lots of sparkle, decorative stitches look well worked with Snow. It is available in white in 10 yd. skeins and 40 yd. cards.

Ultra Suede (Rainbow Gallery) A 100% polyester and polyurethane thread, made in Japan, that provides a suede-like effect. Use short lengths and stitch gently as the thread is easily broken. Lay the thread on both sides of the canvas to avoid twisting. Ultra Suede is available in 47 colors. (These colors depend on the fashion industry and therefore are not always available.) Nine basic colors (white, black, red, grays and tans) are always stocked. Ultra Suede is packaged on cards of five 1 yd. lengths.

Velour 18 Shadowdyed (Needle Necessities, Inc.) Velour Fine Mesh, a 100% nylon thread is shadowdyed to produce a tone-on-tone coloration. Stitching with this thread creates the look of velvet. This thread comes in 5 yd. packages and is available in 24 colors named after precious jewels.

Velour Fine Mesh (Fleur de Paris) A 100% nylon thread that works perfectly for basketweave on 18 mesh canvas. When stitched this thread gives the effect of velvet. The manufacturer states that dye lot variations are significant; therefore, purchase enough to complete a project. Color fastness is not guaranteed, so treat carefully when blocking and finishing. This thread is available in 68 colors and is sold in 10 yd. blister packages.

WOOL

Alpaca 18 (Rainbow Gallery) A 100% alpaca thread, made in Peru. It can be brushed with a Bunka Brush or tooth brush to maximize its furry effect. It is available in 17 natural animal colors in 12 yd. cards.

Appleton Crewel Wool (Access Commodities) A single strand wool that is imported from England and has a marvelous range of shades in each color. The number of strands can be increased to provide excellent coverage on 8 to 24 mesh canvas. This thread is available in 421 colors and is packaged in skeins (30 meters) or hanks (approx. 195 yds.).

Broider Wul (Access Commodities) A wonderfully soft, fine 100% wool that is hand-dyed with natural dyes and is imported from England. This thread was chiefly created for the restoration of needlework dated before 1840, however, it can be used for any type of needlework. It is available in 99 colors that range from rich and brilliant dark colors to soft and subtle lighter colors. This wool is packaged in 30 yd. skeins and 300 yd. hanks.

Designer's Dream (Rainbow Gallery) A hand washable, 100% virgin wool made in Italy. It is packaged in 30 yd. cards and is available in 65 colors.

EPiC Worsted 99 Line Multitone (Excellent Production in Craft, Inc.) Formerly known as Dimin Multitone, EPiC is a 2-ply worsted wool that is available in 99 colors. Each color has multiple tones which, when stitched, create a tweeded effect. EPiC can be used alone or combined with other threads. It is available in 1 or 2 oz. hanks.

Faux Fur (Rainbow Gallery) This 85% acrylic, 15% wool thread has a furry appearance and is made in Italy. Stitch carefully in short lengths with a larger than normal size needle to keep the thread from falling apart. Faux Fur is available in 12 colors on 20 yd. cards.

French Wool Overdyed (Needle Necessities, Inc.) A fine, 100% virgin wool yarn that has been overdyed by hand, resulting in a subtle, shaded effect. These are overdyed threads generally of the same color family. Combine this thread with a complementary solid color for a tweeded effect. To obtain a mottled or tweeded effect, reverse some of the strands. This thread is packaged in 37 yd. skeins and is available in 50 colors.

Medici Wool (DMC Corporation) A 100% virgin wool made in France. It is a particularly soft wool and multiple strands may be used to obtain good coverage on most sizes of canvas or fabric. This wool is available in 27.3 yd. skeins in 180 colors.

Paternayan Persian Wool (JCA Inc.) A fine 100% virgin wool available in 405 colors in 68 color families. It is a 3-ply easily divisible wool sold in 8 yd. skeins and 4 oz. hanks. Some shops also sell Paternayan by the strand.

Santa's Beard & Suit (Rainbow Gallery) An 85% acrylic, 15% wool thread that is made in Italy. It has a furry appearance. Stitch carefully in short lengths with a larger than normal size needle to keep the thread from falling apart. It is available in 7 colors in 10 yd. cards.

Twedie 18 (Rainbow Gallery) A 100% wool thread made in England. As its name implies, this thread gives a tweeded effect without the need to combine multiple strands of different colors in the needle. Twedie can also be brushed for a fuzzy effect. It is available in 15 yd. cards in 36 colors.

Wisper (Rainbow Gallery) A fuzzy thread which is 70% kid mohair and 30% nylon. The nylon is included to provide strength to the thread. Wisper can be used alone or combined with another thin strand wool. It can also be brushed to provide a fuller effect. It is made in Italy and is available in 37 colors on 20 yd. cards.

THREAD TO CANVAS/FABRIC CONVERSION CHART

THREAD	13/14 CANVAS	18 CANVAS	22/24 CANVAS	28 FABRIC
Alpaca 18	1	1	-	-
Antica	-	1	-	-
Appleton Crewel Wool	3	2	1	1
Backgrounds Helene	-	1	-	-
Backgrounds Natural Flax	1	1*		-
Backgrounds Natural Linen	-	1	-	-
Backgrounds Natural Silk	1	1*	-	-
Backgrounds Silk & Cream	1	1*	-	-
Bravo!	5 P	3 P	2 P	1 P
Broider Wul	4-5	2-3	1	1
Candlelight	2	1-2	-	-
Charleston	1	1	-	-
Cotton Embroidery Floss	8 P	5 P	3 P	2 P
Cresta d'Oro	2	1	-	-
Crystal Rays	1	1*	-	-
Designer's Dream	4	2	1	1
Double Dipped Rachel	1	1*	-	-
Empress Silk	6	4 P	2 P	2 P
EPiC	3	2	1	1
Encore!	3-4 P	2 P	1 P	1 P
Faux Fur	1	-	-	-
Fiesta!	6 P	4 P	1 P	2 P
Flair	1	1	1*	-
Floche	4	2	1-2	1
Floss Overdyed	8 P	5 P	3 P	2 P
Flower Thread	6	3	1	1
French Wool Overdyed	5	3	2	1
Frosty Rays	1	1*	1*	-
Fyre Werks	1	1	1*	1
Gold Rush 14	1	-	-	-
Gold Rush 18	-	1	1	1
Impressions	2	1	1	1

P Ply
* Use for long stitches

THREAD TO CANVAS/FABRIC CONVERSION CHART
(continued)

THREAD	13/14 CANVAS	18 CANVAS	22/24 CANVAS	28 FABRIC
Kit Kin	4	2	1	1
Kreinik Very Fine (#4) Braid	-	-	1	1
Kreinik Fine (#8) Braid	-	1	1	1
Kreinik Medium (#16) Braid	1-2	1	-	-
Kreinik Heavy (#32) Braid	1	-	-	-
Kreinik 1/8" Ribbon	1	-	-	-
Kreinik 1/16" Ribbon	-	1	1*	-
Kreinik Cord	-	-	6	4
Kreinik Ombre	-	-	1	-
Kreinik Silk Mori	6 P	3 P	2 P	2 P
Kreinik Silk Serica	-	1	-	-
Lacquered Jewels	-	8	6	-
Madras	8	4-8	2-3	1-2
Marlitt	6 P	4 P	1 P	2 P
Matte 18	-	1	-	-
Matte Cotton	1	-	-	-
Medici Wool	6-7	3	2	1
Metallic Ribbon Floss	1	1	1*	-
Moon Glow	2	1	1*	-
Neon Rays	1	1	1*	1
Overture	2 P	1 P	-	1
Patent Leather	1	1*	-	-
Paternayan Persian Wool	2	1	1	1
Patina	1	1	2 P	3 P
Pearl 8 Overdyed	-	-	1	1
Pearl Cotton #3	1	-	-	-
Pearl Cotton #5	-	1	-	-
Pearl Cotton #8	-	1	1	1
Pearl Cotton #12	-	-	1	1
Pebbly Perle	1	1	2 P	2 P
Per"Suede"	1	1*	1*	-
Pizzaz	-	1	1	1

P Ply
* Use for long stitches

THREAD TO CANVAS/FABRIC CONVERSION CHART
(continued)

THREAD	13/14 CANVAS	18 CANVAS	22/24 CANVAS	28 FABRIC
Pure & Simple	2	1	-	-
Rachel	1	1	1*	-
Rachel Solid	1	1	1*	-
Rachel Overdyed	1	1	1*	-
Rachelette	1	1*	-	-
Rainbow Linen	-	1	1	1
Rayon Ribbon Floss	1	1	1*	-
Reflection Collection	2	1	1	1
Rhapsody	1	1	1*	-
Santa's Beard & Suit	1	-	-	-
Shimmer	2	1	1*	-
Silk/Wool	5 P	3 P	2 P	1-2 P
Snow	-	1	1*	-
Soie Cristale	6 P	4 P	2 P	1-2 P
Soie d'Alger	7 P	4 P	2 P	1 P
Splendor	6 P	4 P	2 P	1 P
Spring II	2	1	-	-
Spring II Shadowdyed	2	1	-	-
Sprinkles	2	1	1*	-
Super Twist	-	8	6	4
Tiara	2	1	1*	1
Trebizond	2	1	1*	-
Twedie 18	2	1	-	-
Ultra Sprinkles	2	1	1*	-
Ultra Suede	1	1*	-	-
Velour 18 Shadowdyed	2	1	1*	-
Velour Fine Mesh	2	1	1*	-
Watercolours	2 P	1 P	1 P*	-
Waterlilies	6 P	4 P	2 P	1-2 P
Wildflowers	3	2	1	1
Wisper	4	2	1	1

P Ply
* Use for long stitches

MANUFACTURERS AND DISTRIBUTORS CHART

The following list of wholesale manufacturers and distributors has been provided so that you can find retail sources for the threads listed in this book.

Access Commodities
P.O. Box 1995
Rowlett, TX 75030

> Appleton Wool
> Broider Wul
> Soie d'Alger
> Trebizond

Anchor (Division of Susan Bates)
30 Patewood Drive
Greenville, SC 29615

> Cotton Embroidery Floss
> Pearl Cotton #3, #5, #8, #12
> Marlitt

the CARON Collection
67 Poland Street
Bridgeport, CT 06605

> Antica
> Candlelight
> Double Dipped Rachel
> Impressions
> Kit Kin
> Rachel
> Rachelette
> Snow
> Soie Cristale
> Watercolours
> Waterlilies
> Wildflowers

DMC Corporation
10 Port Kearny
South Kearny, NJ 07032

> Cotton Embroidery Floss
> Flower Thread
> Medici Wool
> Pearl Cotton #3, #5, #8, #12

Designing Women, Unltd.
601 East Eighth Street
El Dorado, AR 71730

> Metallic Ribbon Floss
> Rayon Ribbon Floss
> Reflection Collection

Excellent Production in Craft, Inc
P.O. Box 1218
Waldoboro, ME 04572-1218

> EPiC Worsted 99 Line Multitone

Fleur de Paris, Inc.
5835 Washington Boulevard
Culver City, CA 90230

> Velour Fine Mesh

JCA Inc.
35 Scales Lane
Townsend, MA 01469

> Paternayan Wool

J. L. Walsh Inc.
4338 Edgewood
Oakland, CA 94602

> Silk/Wool

Julia Golson Designs
490 Forestdale Drive
Atlanta, GA 30342

> Floche

Kreinik Manufacturing Company Inc.
3106 Timanus Lane, Suite #101
Baltimore, MD 21244

Kreinik Very Fine (#4) Braid
Kreinik Fine (#8) Braid
Kreinik Medium (#16) Braid
Kreinik Heavy (#32) Braid
Kreinik $1/8$" Ribbon
Kreinik $1/16$" Ribbon
Kreinik Cord
Kreinik Ombre
Kreinik Silk Mori
Kreinik Silk Serica
Soie d'Alger

Needle Necessities, Inc.
14746 N.E. 95th St.
Redmond, WA 98052

Charleston
Empress Silk
Floss Overdyed
French Wool Overdyed
Madras
Pearl 8 Overdyed
Rachel Overdyed
Rachel Solid
Spring II
Spring II Shadowdyed
Velour 18 Shadowdyed

Rainbow Gallery
7412 Fulton Avenue, #5
North Hollywood, CA 91605

Alpaca 18
Backgrounds Helene
Backgrounds Natural Flax
Backgrounds Natural Linen
Backgrounds Natural Silk
Backgrounds Silk & Cream
Bravo!
Cresta d'Oro

Crystal Rays
Designer's Dream
Encore!
Faux Fur
Fiesta!
Flair
Frosty Rays
Fyre Werks
Gold Rush 14
Gold Rush 18
Matte 18
Neon Rays
Overture
Patent Leather
Patina
Pebbly Perle
Rainbow Linen
Rhapsody
Santa's Beard & Suit
Splendor
Tiara
Twedie 18
Ultra Suede
Wisper

Renaissance Designs

15 Rogers Road
Far Hills, NJ 07931

Moon Glow
Per"Suede"
Pizzaz
Pure & Simple
Shimmer
Sprinkles
Ultra Sprinkles

Sarah Bennett Specialties
11879 Walton Lake Road
Disputanta, VA 23842

Lacquered Jewels
Super Twist

We would like to express our thanks to the aforementioned thread manufacturers and distributors for permission to use their thread information.

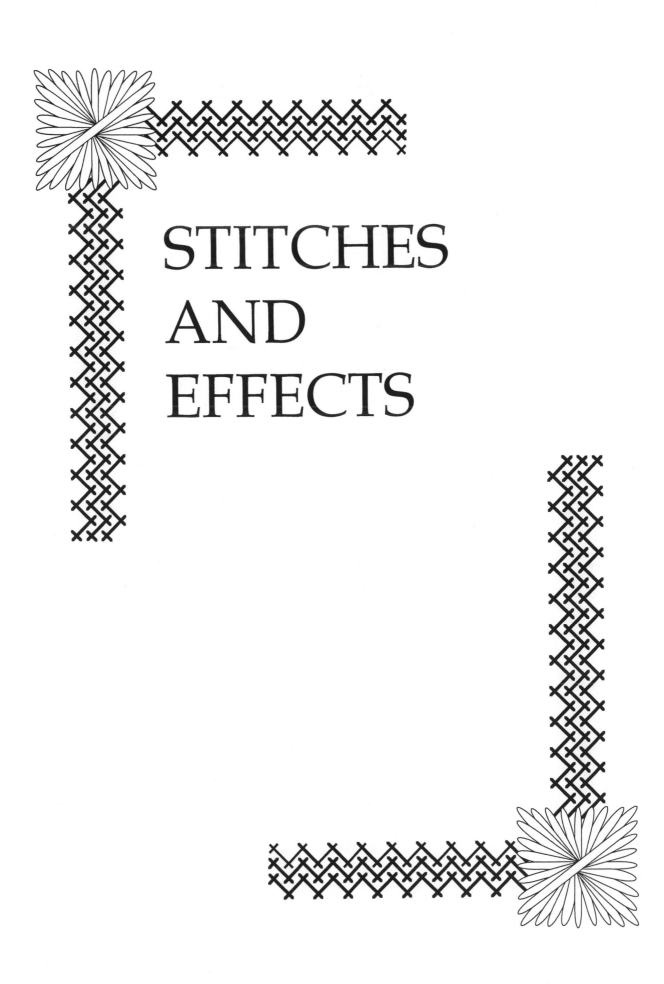

STITCHES AND EFFECTS

ALICIA'S LACE: This lacy, open stitch is very versatile. It gives the effect of pulled work without the effort. This stitch is excellent for lacy dresses, petticoats, and ruffles. It is an effective background when you want a textured or open look because it does not completely cover the canvas. For a very open background, choose a thread that is too thin to solidly cover your canvas ground such as #8 or #12 pearl cotton on 18 mesh canvas. Try matching your thread color to your canvas color. After you have completed the diamond portion of the stitch, use a contrasting thread such as a metallic, overdyed, or rayon to fill in each diamond with a short running stitch. For instance, if you have used Watercolours in your piece, use the same color in Wildflowers for the running stitch in your background.

ALTERNATING CONTINENTAL (Alternating Tent): This stitch is very effective for clothing details such as sweater ribbing, hems, and cuffs as well as hats, and mittens. Sweaters, hats, and mittens usually look more realistic when stitched in wool, wool blends or cotton; however, ribbon and rayon thread also make marvelous clothing. Think of this stitch for angel wings and butterfly wings. Use a soft metallic such as Candlelight, Tiara, or a Kreinik #4 or #8 braid for an ethereal wing effect. This is also an excellent background stitch which does not completely cover the canvas. This stitch works very well for small pieces that just need slight coverage. Choose a light colored thread or a thread finer than usual for coverage on your ground size.

ALTERNATING OBLONG CROSS (Encroaching Oblong Cross): This is another excellent clothing stitch. The light play on your thread sometimes looks as though you have used more than one shade, especially when using silk. Coats, jackets, and dresses are fabulous in this stitch. Consider using two close color values to really add depth to your piece. Tightly twisted threads such as pearl cotton and Trebizond are not as effective in this stitch. Try softer twist threads such as Kreinik Silk Serica, Watercolours, Encore!, Matte 18, Pebbly Perle, stranded cotton or silk; or Medici Wool, Appleton Crewel, EPiC, or Broider Wul. This is also a good stitch for landscapes, shrubs, and architectural columns; try an overdyed thread with appropriate coverage for your ground size.

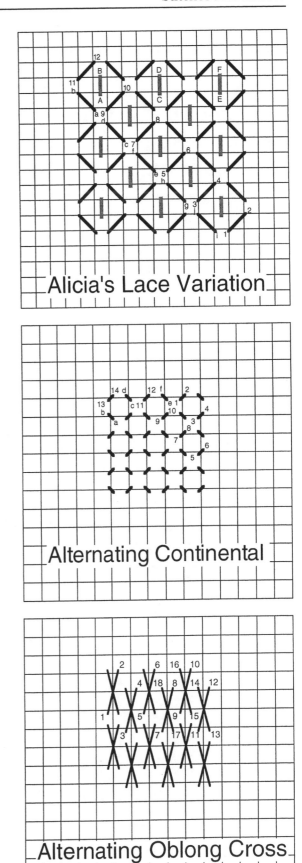

Alicia's Lace Variation

Alternating Continental

Alternating Oblong Cross

ALTERNATING SMYRNA CROSS: This stitch gives a very realistic look to garlands, window box greenery, and wreaths. Also consider it for small bushes or the tops of distant trees. It is especially effective when stitched with an overdyed thread such as Wildflowers, Watercolours, Encore!, or Floss Overdyed. It gives a wonderful pebbly look to cobblestone walks, country stone walls, or roughly paved streets. Here again, overdyed threads are very effective, and the use of an overdyed thread eliminates the need for shading in these areas.

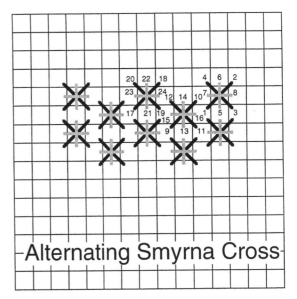

Alternating Smyrna Cross

BARGELLO LINE PATTERN #1: The use of bargello, or Florentine, patterns in designs can be considered for many different areas. Mountains, sunsets, and ocean waves are just a few of the landscape and seascape potentials. In these instances an overdyed thread gives a stunning effect. This pattern is lovely in long Santa's robes, especially in overdyed wool or silk such as French Wool Overdyed or Waterlilies. It can also be quite effective in small pieces of clothing because it is easy to compensate. As a background, this stitch pattern can be bold or subdued depending upon your choice of color. Use pale values of one or more colors for a very subtle look. Use dark hues of colors that complement your piece for a bold effect.

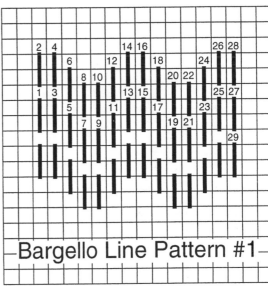

Bargello Line Pattern #1

BARGELLO LINE PATTERN #2 (see Bargello Line Pattern #1): This stitch is very effective not only for backgrounds, but also works well for clothing, sky, and even large Christmas bells.

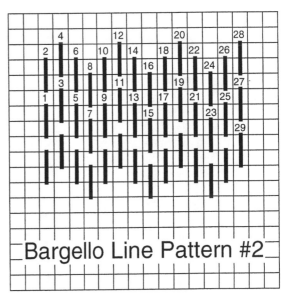

Bargello Line Pattern #2

BRICK: This simple stitch creates an incredibly versatile effect, and it can be used either horizontally or vertically. It is marvelous for sky, lakes, and lawns particularly when stitched with an overdyed thread. Also consider using this stitch horizontally for belts on Santas or nutcrackers. When stitched in Ultra Suede or Per"Suede" it looks like a woven leather belt. It is also quite effective with Neon Rays or Ribbon Floss. This is also a very good background stitch and works well with either single strand or multi-ply thread. If you are using multiple plies, be sure to carefully lay the thread for the best effect.

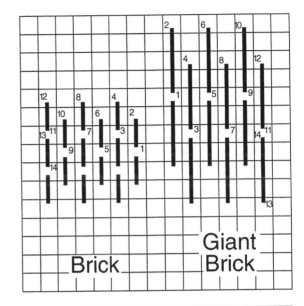

Brick

Giant Brick

BROAD CROSS: This very effective stitch should be used in large areas since the stitch unit is 6 threads high and 6 threads wide. It gives a raised effect and, therefore, can be wonderful for the hat of a large nutcracker. The use of Spring II or Rainbow Linen produces a striking woven effect for baskets or even Santa's bag. For clothing, use threads with a sheen like pearl cotton, a rayon such as Patina, or silk. This stitch works for stone walls, cobblestones, and wide sidewalks. Try matte cotton, Matte 18, or Pebbly Perle for a more realistic look.

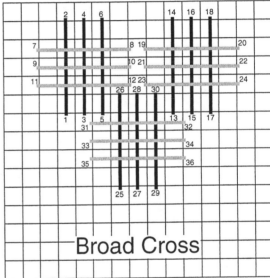

Broad Cross

BURDEN STITCH: This stitch is one of the basic units in laid fillings, and can be used in many different combinations. It is usually easier to work with 2 threaded needles, couching the laid threads as you go along. For an elegant Christmas tree, lay a metallic braid for the ground thread and couch over it with an overdyed thread such as Watercolours, Wildflowers, Encore!, Bravo, or French Wool Overdyed. This stitch can be compensated to fit a design area by shortening and/or elongating the length of your laid ground threads. For Santa's bag or a distinctive basket try other combinations such as Rainbow Linen mixed with wool or pearl cotton; or combine Spring II, matte cotton or Matte 18 with Patina or Marlitt; or use Sprinkles with Pure & Simple.

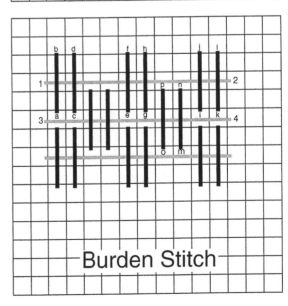

Burden Stitch

BYZANTINE #1: This is a wonderful background stitch which completely covers the canvas and creates a stair-like effect. It is also good for filling in diagonal areas. In large areas, it makes an interesting border on clothing, but isn't very effective in small areas. Choose a metallic ribbon to work a background for a very special piece. Stranded cotton or silk or any overdyed thread gives a marvelous effect. If you choose an overdyed thread, try reversing some of the plies for a more mottled appearance.

BYZANTINE #2: This stitch variation is also good for backgrounds. It creates a striking night sky, especially with a dark metallic ribbon. Distant mountains come to life when stitched in stranded cotton or even a very subtle overdyed thread. Try this stitch for rivers and roads, too. Tightly twisted threads such as pearl cotton or Trebizond silk do not give good coverage with this stitch. Use a thread with multiple plies or one with a looser twist. Also, consider using one of the nylon threads such as Rachel, Rachelette, Flair, or Frosty Rays.

BYZANTINE SCOTCH: Use this stitch to create a wonderful stone fireplace or wall. Also, consider using it for garden walls, paths or roads. Any of the overdyed threads are ideal here. You achieve a shaded effect without having to change the thread in your needle, especially if you reverse the plies. Also an effective background in a simple piece, the result is subtle when stitched in a pale color or bold in a medium or dark value. This stitch can be overwhelming, so use it carefully for backgrounds. In the right place it provides a dynamic effect.

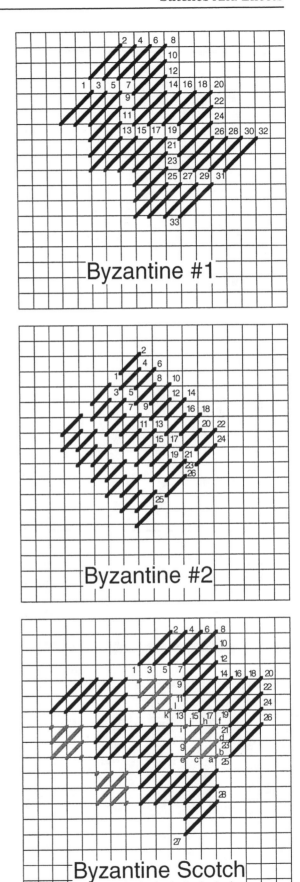

Byzantine #1

Byzantine #2

Byzantine Scotch

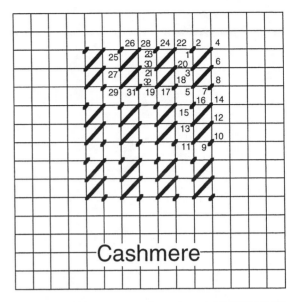

Cashmere

CASHMERE: This is one of the most versatile of all stitches. It works well in large as well as small areas and is easy to compensate. Consider this stitch for brick houses. It fits well as window molding, door panels, and shutters. It also creates very realistic brick walls, walkways, and chimneys. Any of the overdyed threads are terrific for houses as they produce a shaded effect without a lot of effort. Pearl cotton, matte cotton, Matte 18, and Pebbly Perle are also very effective for architectural detailing.

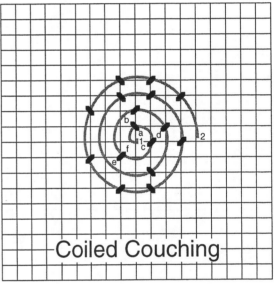

Coiled Couching

COILED COUCHING: This is a surface embroidery stitch that can be adapted for canvas work. It creates a very distinctive beard for Santa or curly hair. You need to work with two needles to complete this stitch. Use a heavy thread such as Santa's Beard & Suit, Persian wool, or tapestry wool for the coils. Be bold with your choice of a couching thread. Think about the finer metallic threads such as Pizzaz, Kreinik Very Fine (#4) Braid, or Kreinik Cord. You could even try Medici Wool, Designer's Dream, or Wisper for the couching thread. To complete the effect of Coiled Couching, fill in the uncovered areas between coils with French Knots.

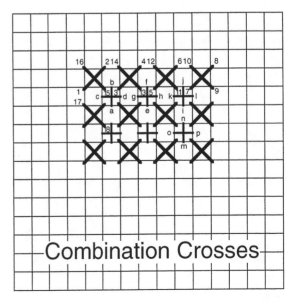

Combination Crosses

COMBINATION CROSSES (Interlocked Upright & Diagonal Cross Stitch): This is another stitch that works in small areas and is easy to compensate. It is especially effective for clothing. Twisted silks such as Trebizond and Kreinik Silk Serica produce a shiny satin look as does pearl cotton. Wool, stranded cotton, matte cotton, Matte 18, and Pebbly Perle look flatter and duller. This can be another great opportunity to try an overdyed thread.

CROSS PLUS TWO: This stitch produces different effects with different threads. The use of pearl cotton, Trebizond, Kreinik Silk Serica, Bravo, Wildflowers, Encore!, or Pearl 8 Overdyed produces a very lacy, open canvas effect. If you stitch with Medici Wool, Designer's Dream, Persian wool, or crewel wool the appearance is much heavier and covers the canvas. If you choose to use fewer strands of wool, you also create a lace-like effect. Consider this stitch for backgrounds, taking into account your thread choice and the effect you want to achieve, light or heavy coverage.

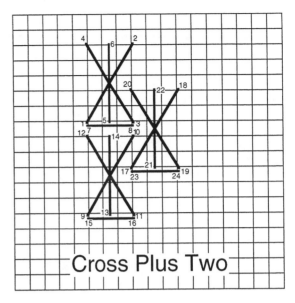

Cross Plus Two

CUSHION STITCH (Framed Scotch, Scottish): This is a fine background stitch, especially if stitched in two different threads. Consider using Rachel for the Scotch unit and a matching color in metallic ribbon for the tent stitches; Impressions with the matching color in Soie Cristale; or Watercolours or Overture with a coordinating pearl cotton. The combinations are limited only by your imagination. When choosing this stitch, make sure your background complements and does not overwhelm your piece.

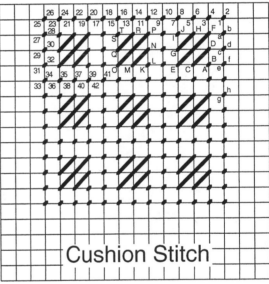

Cushion Stitch

DAMASK: As the name implies, this stitch looks like damask and is wonderful for clothing. Try using Floche, stranded cotton, Soie Cristale, Splendor, or Soie d'Alger. This is an excellent background stitch that works well in almost any thread, even a metallic thread such as Frye Werks or one of the Kreinik Ribbons.

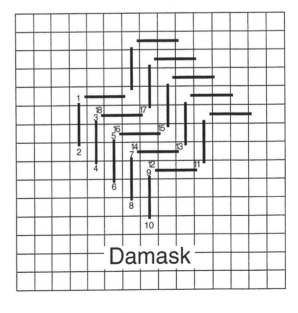

Damask

DARNING PATTERNS: These openwork patterns are a fabulous background option for the stitcher who doesn't need heavy coverage. All the patterns are worked in an over-under method, starting with an away waste knot and leave a tail to be ended outside the body of the piece.

Most of these patterns are worked in straight lines, but we have included one diagonal pattern.

Think of these patterns to create snow, sky, grass, or water. They also make great backgrounds for pieces that may be finished as standing dolls.

Metallic threads like Tiara, Pizzaz, Candlelight, Gold Rush, or one of the Kreinik Braids work very well in darning patterns. They add shimmer and shine to a piece, giving just a hint of coverage. The metallics are extremely effective for stitching snow scenes, or a snowy background. Consider lining the piece with a shiny fabric such as lame to increase the sparkle and add dimension of the darning pattern background.

Softly twisted threads like pearl cotton, especially the finer sizes, are very effective. Try #5 pearl cotton for 13/14 mesh or #8 or #12 pearl cotton for 18 mesh canvas. To create a very subtle look, try to match the pearl cotton color to your canvas or fabric color.

This is another place to use the finer sizes of the overdyed threads such as Wildflowers, Bravo! and Pearl 8 Overdyed. Also consider using variegated pearl cotton for sky or water.

The twisted silks and rayons such as Trebizond, Kreinik Silk Mori, and Patina will also work well in these darning patterns. These threads will shine more than pearl cotton and add elegance to the piece.

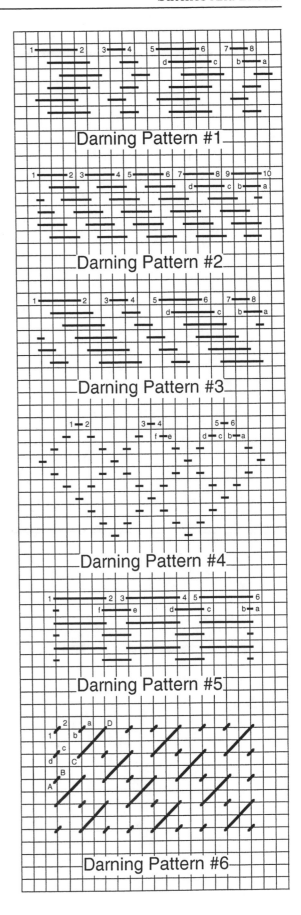

Darning Pattern #1

Darning Pattern #2

Darning Pattern #3

Darning Pattern #4

Darning Pattern #5

Darning Pattern #6

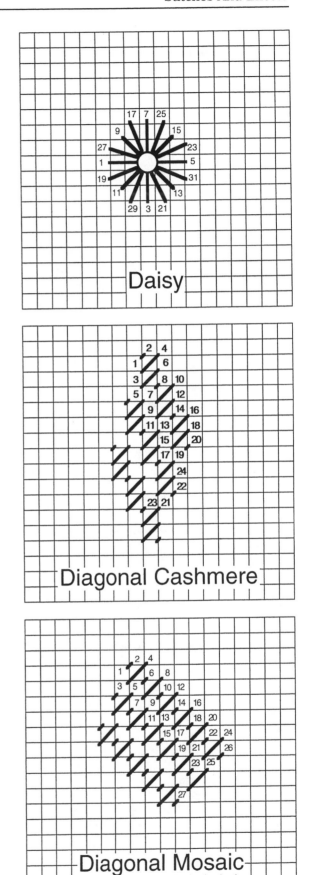

Daisy

Diagonal Cashmere

Diagonal Mosaic

DAISY: This eyelet variation creates lacy dresses, animal eyes, flowers or snowflakes. An overdyed thread such as Wildflowers, Bravo, Waterlilies, Pearl 8 Overdyed, or Floss Overdyed is very effective for flowers. Try using a stranded cotton, Floche, pearl cotton, matte cotton, or Matte 18 for clothing. Any of the Kreinik metallic braids, Tiara, Candlelight, Antica, Lacquered Jewels, or Kreinik Cord are also very effective in this stitch. Kreinik Cord gives a wet, shiny look that can be very realistic for animal eyes. Try Tiara, Candlelight, Antica, or Snow for snowflakes.

DIAGONAL CASHMERE (Continuous Cashmere): This stitch is wonderful for area rugs and carpets, especially when stitched in wool. Also think of this stitch for clothing such as coats and flowing capes. When stitching articles of clothing, first consider the look you want to achieve, then choose your thread. Shiny threads such as Trebizond, Kreinik Silk Serica, Floche, Neon Rays, and Ribbon Floss create elegant clothing. Matte threads such as stranded cotton, matte cotton, Matte 18, Rainbow Linen, and wool produce a softer, more subtle look. This is also a fine background stitch, as it gives good coverage, is easy to compensate and moves very quickly.

DIAGONAL MOSAIC (Continuous Mosaic, Diagonal Florentine, Small Diagonal): This versatile stitch fits into small areas and also works well as a background. Use this stitch for both water and sky, with an overdyed thread. It is great for any article of clothing, especially cuffs and collars. Also consider this stitch for large areas of grass or fields. It is also good for angel and butterfly wings. With the use of a metallic thread such as Candlelight, Tiara, or Kreinik Braid, an ethereal effect is created. Create flowing ribbons by changing the stitch direction on each side of the ribbon using shiny flat thread such as Neon Rays or Ribbon Floss. For a background try alternating rows with different threads of the same color such as Soie Cristale and Impressions, Neon Rays and Flair, or wool and pearl cotton. Another option is to use two close values of one stranded cotton color. Use Watercolours or Overture with a corresponding pearl cotton, Floche, or stranded cotton for a very dramatic effect.

DIAGONAL SCOTCH (Large Diagonal): This is another very effective background stitch. It covers the canvas well and moves very quickly. Like the Diagonal Mosaic, this stitch can be worked in two threads, alternating each row. Consider two close values of one stranded cotton color, or combine two threads of the same color such as Soie Cristale with Impressions, Rachel with Rachelette, or wool with pearl cotton. You may also use this stitch for large articles of clothing such as coats and capes. If you are stitching both sides of a coat or cape, consider changing the stitch direction, the right side slanted to the right and the left side slanted to the left. This gives some curve and movement to the garment. This stitch also works for seaweed, large leaves, or large tree tops.

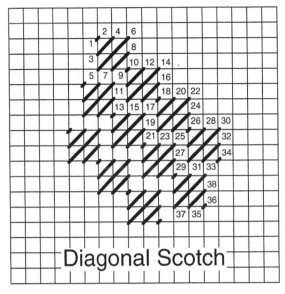

Diagonal Scotch

DIAMOND EYELET (Diamond Star Stitch): This is a wonderful stitch for flower gardens or for individual flowers on a stem. If you are using it for individual flowers, eliminate the tent outline around each motif. Consider embellishing each motif by attaching a bead in the center. Flowers are effective in most of the shiny threads such as pearl cotton, Trebizond, Floche, Kreinik Silk Serica or any stranded silk such as Soie Cristale, Kreinik Silk Mori, Soie d'Alger, or Splendor.

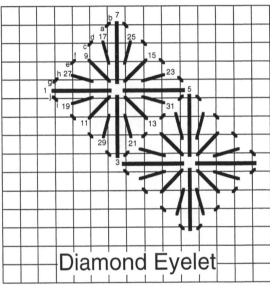

Diamond Eyelet

DIAMOND RAY: This stitch looks like a small leaf and can be worked both diagonally and horizontally. It is perfect for large Christmas wreaths, long garlands, small bushes, flower box greenery or as an individual leaf on a flower stem. This is another great place to use an overdyed thread. Finer threads such as Wildflowers, Waterlilies, Pearl 8 Overdyed, Floss Overdyed, or Bravo! are the most effective since they are thin enough to show each of the stitch elements. If you are using 13/14 mesh canvas, consider using 1 ply of Watercolours or Overture.

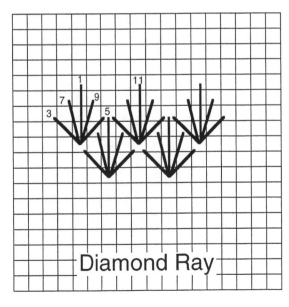

Diamond Ray

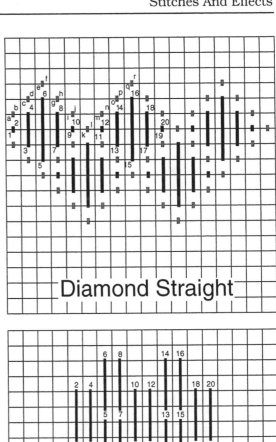

Diamond Straight

DIAMOND STRAIGHT: This stitch creates a textured look for paths, roads, walkways, and mountains. It also creates very interesting flowers. Any of the overdyed threads work well, as does pearl cotton, wool, matte cotton, Matte 18, Pebbly Perle or Rainbow Linen. This stitch is especially effective for clothing in Spring II or Floche. It is also an excellent background stitch.

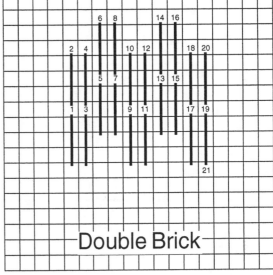

Double Brick

DOUBLE BRICK: This is another very versatile stitch that can be used both horizontally and vertically. It works well for landscapes, houses, walls, walkways, roads, grass, and chimneys. Stranded cotton or silk is very effective in this stitch since it spreads to cover the canvas. Be sure to lay your threads so they look even. Overdyed thread, particularly Floss Overdyed, Waterlilies, and Bravo! create gorgeous lawns, fields, sky, oceans, and lakes. When stitching these areas with overdyed thread, try reversing some of the plies in your needle to give a mottled or tweeded look to your piece. This is also an excellent background stitch that is effective in almost every available thread.

DOUBLE STITCH: This stitch creates a wonderful texture for bushes, large shrubs, tree trunks, and Christmas trees. Use a solid color for the large cross and a fine overdyed thread for the small cross, or use two different threads of the same color. Use Pure & Simple for the large cross and Sprinkles for the small cross to obtain a lighted Christmas tree effect. You could even mix a wool such as Medici, EPiC, Appleton Crewel, or Designer's Dream with a metallic braid such as Kreinik Very Fine (#4) Braid, Kreinik Fine (#8) Braid, Tiara, or Gold Rush 18. Another place to consider this stitch is for Santa's boots. Use pearl cotton, Floche or Patina for a glossy look, or try one of the metallic braids such as Kreinik Very Fine (#4) Braid, Kreinik Fine (#8) Braid, Tiara, or Gold Rush 18. For fur trim on a coat try using a neutral overdyed thread, wool or pearl cotton.

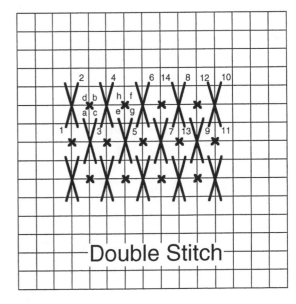

Double Stitch

DOUBLE STRAIGHT CROSS (Double Cross Stitch): This is a great stitch for crowns. A metallic braid such as Kreinik Fine (#8) Braid or Kreinik Medium (#16) Braid gives the effect of gold filigree. It is also wonderful for the moon and stars. Use a metallic thread such as Tiara, Gold Rush 18, Kreinik Very Fine (#4) Braid, Kreinik Fine (#8) Braid, or Snow. There is a lacy look to ruffles and petticoats when you choose a fine thread such as #8 or #12 pearl cotton.

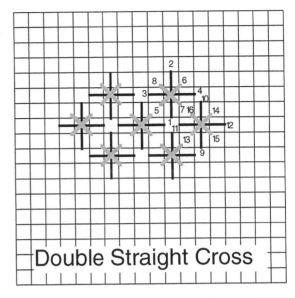

Double Straight Cross

ENCROACHING OBLIQUE: This is a very versatile stitch that creates a slanted straight line. It works well for wall molding, paths, grass, and stucco walls. It also creates a very distinctive border or a decorative dividing border for the top or in the body of Christmas stockings. Use stranded cotton or silk for architectural accents. Consider Neon Rays or Ribbon Floss, Wildflowers, Pearl 8 Overdyed, or Bravo! for decorative borders. This stitch creates very effective eyebrows, especially in wool, wool combined with Wisper or Kit Kin, or Santa's Beard and Suit.

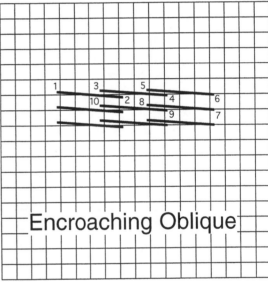

Encroaching Oblique

FAN VAULTING: This is a very effective background stitch that provides different coverage depending on your thread and ground choice. The use of pearl cotton, Watercolours, Trebizond or Pebbly Perle creates a lacy look with open canvas. If you use a stranded wool such as Persian, Medici, or Appleton Crewel, or a thicker thread such as matte cotton or Matte 18, you create a heavier and very different look.

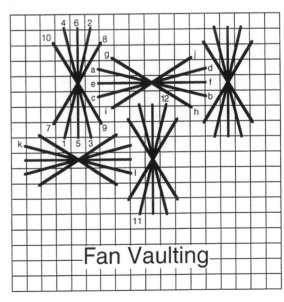

Fan Vaulting

FLYING CROSS: This diagonal stitch creates wonderful effects in clothing. Try using wool, stranded cotton or silk, or pearl cotton, matte cotton, Pure & Simple, Spring II, Trebizond or Kreinik Silk Serica. This is also an excellent background stitch.

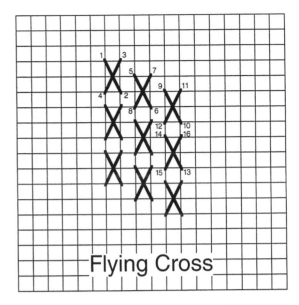

Flying Cross

FRAMED PAVILLION: This is a marvelous stitch for clothing, especially long Santa's robes and elaborate dresses. Stitch the diamond shape in wool, EPiC, Impressions, Soie Cristale, or Silk/Wool. Complete the long stitch in a coordinating metallic such as Kreinik Very Fine (#4) or Fine (#8) Braid, Lacquered Jewels, Pizzaz, Tiara, or Candlelight. Use the same shade or choose another color from the piece to highlight this area. You may even want to alternate the colors in each row of the diamond shaped pavillions. This is an excellent background stitch, either in thread combinations or all in the same thread.

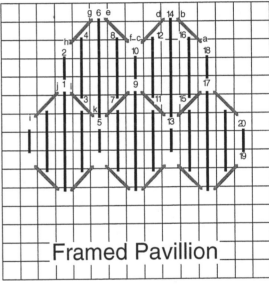

Framed Pavillion

GIANT DIAGONAL SCOTCH (Continuous Flat Stitch): This is an excellent background stitch. It covers large areas well and moves quickly. It creates spectacular sky, oceans, or mountains. Try this stitch in any of the overdyed threads for landscape or seascape scenes. If your design is stitched with pearl cotton, try wool or matte cotton for the background to contrast the textures. Your imagination is the "only limit" for all of these suggestions.

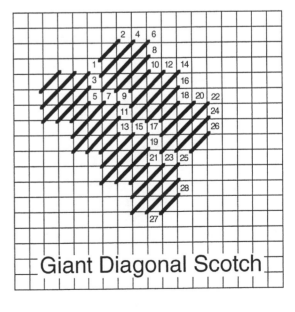

Giant Diagonal Scotch

GOBELIN: This stitch is your workhorse and can be used almost any place. It creates wonderful details and is the stitch to use when nothing else works. Use it either vertically or horizontally. It can cover 2, 3, or 4 canvas threads depending upon your needs. Whenever you have a space over two threads, consider using this stitch. The Gobelin stitch is quite effective in stranded cotton or silk, Floche, Medici, Broider Wul, and Appleton Crewel. It is also very effective stitched in Ribbon Floss or Neon Rays (be sure to lay it carefully). Pearl cotton, matte cotton, Matte 18, Pebbly Perle, Pure & Simple, or Sprinkles also work very well. This is the ideal stitch for Per"Suede" and Ultra Suede. When using these two threads, be sure they lay flat on both the front and back of the canvas.

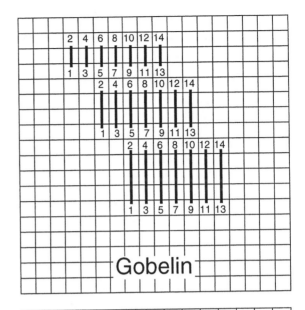

Gobelin

HALF DROP RHODES: This interestingly textured stitch creates a unique effect. Try it for fish scales, especially in a shiny thread such as Trebizond, pearl cotton, Sprinkles or Lacquered Jewels. This stitch gives clothing, especially ball gowns or elaborate costumes, a spectacular textured look. Choose a thread that shines such as Sprinkles, Kreinik Silk Serica, Trebizond or pearl cotton.

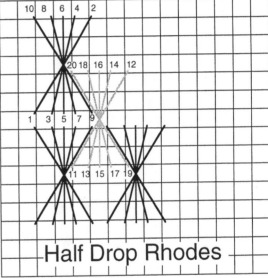

Half Drop Rhodes

HERRINGBONE: This is a great open background stitch for large areas. Try using one of the metallic braids such as Kreinik Very Fine (#4) or Fine (#8) Braid, Tiara or Gold Rush 18 for a look that shimmers. This is also effective stitched in a twisted thread such as pearl cotton or Pebbly Perle, or any of the overdyed threads.

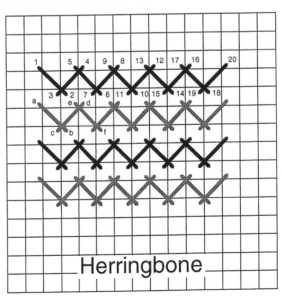

Herringbone

HORIZONTAL ELONGATED SMYRNA: This is an ideal stitch for belt buckles. Use a metallic braid such as Kreinik Fine (#8) Braid or Kreinik Medium (#16) Braid, Tiara, or Gold Rush 18. You could also use matte cotton, Matte 18, or pearl cotton for a matte look. Use this stitch with an overdyed thread such as Watercolours, Overture, or French Wool Overdyed for a cobblestone wall or house.

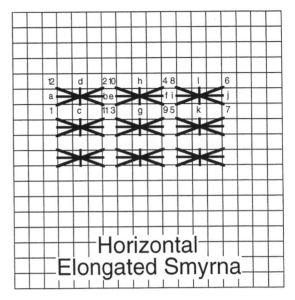

Horizontal Elongated Smyrna

HORIZONTAL MILANESE: This is a great stitch for mountains, especially with one of the textured threads such as Pebbly Perle or Spring II. Use one of the overdyed threads or EPiC for a interestingly shaded mountain effect. Also consider this stitch with an overdyed thread for water in lakes or oceans. This is another good background stitch that covers well and you can use almost any thread available to create a wonderful look.

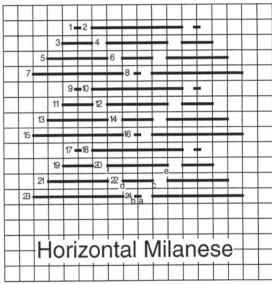

Horizontal Milanese

HORIZONTAL PARISIAN: This is another stitch that works well in small areas and is very easy to compensate. It is very effective for large animals like elephants, as well as for reindeer, horses, and dogs. It creates wonderful bird wings. Try soft threads such as wool, especially French Wool Overdyed, Twedie 18, EPiC, Alpaca 18, or combine wool with Kit Kin or Wisper for a fuzzy animal effect. This is also an excellent background stitch, especially for small pieces.

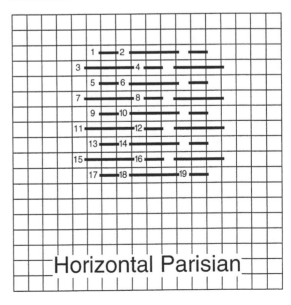

Horizontal Parisian

HUNGARIAN: This is one of the most versatile stitches. It can be worked both vertically and horizontally and looks great in either direction. It is an ideal stitch for clothing, especially Santa's coat, and even for little items since it fits well into small areas. Try stitching the body of a coat, dress, or suit vertically and the sleeves horizontally. Spring II is very effective in this stitch and sometimes looks like velvet. Other good thread choices for clothing are Watercolours, Overture, Wildflowers, Bravo, Soie Cristale, Matte 18, matte cotton, pearl cotton, Floss Overdyed, French Wool Overdyed, Patina, Pure & Simple, Twedie 18, and Rainbow Linen. This stitch is wonderful for backgrounds, either horizontally or vertically.

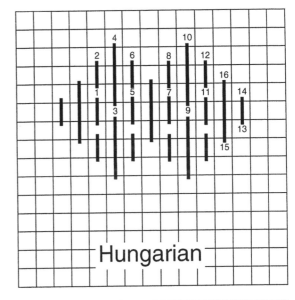

Hungarian

HUNGARIAN GROUND: This variation of the Hungarian stitch is just as versatile as the original. It creates marvelous fish scales, brick patios, walkways, roads, mountains, and is also excellent for clothing. Choose a thread that best represents the area you are stitching; a thread that shimmers such as Tiara, Lacquered Jewels, Sprinkles or Trebizond for fish scales; or less shiny threads, like stranded cotton, Floss Overdyed, Pebbly Perle, Rainbow Linen, matte cotton or Matte 18 for patios, walkways, and roads. This is also an excellent background stitch.

Hungarian Ground

INDIAN STRIPE: This stitch creates very realistic looking denim skirts and prairie skirts, especially with a textured thread such as Spring II or a space-dyed thread like Madras. Another place for this stitch is in Southwestern motifs using a subtle overdyed thread or Madras. You might also use this stitch in geometric designs such as quilts.

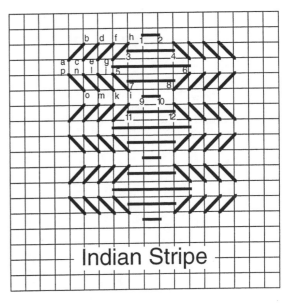

Indian Stripe

IRISH: This stitch is another of the versatile bargello or Florentine patterns that can be considered for many different areas. Use overdyed wool or silk such as French Wool Overdyed or Waterlilies for elegant robes. Mountains, sunsets, and other landscape and seascape areas are also great places to use this stitch. In these instances an overdyed thread gives a stunning effect. This stitch can also be quite effective in small pieces of clothing because it is easy to compensate. As a background, this stitch pattern is bold or subdued depending upon your choice of color. Use pale values of one or more colors for a very subtle look. Use dark hues of colors that complement your piece for a bold effect.

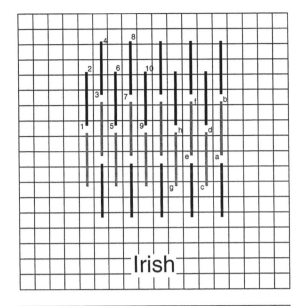

Irish

JACQUARD: This is a great background stitch, especially for a night sky. Try combining two threads in the same color such as Rachel for the longer stitch and one of the Kreinik Ribbons or Fyre Werks for the continental stitch. Other combinations such as Neon Rays and Flair, or Sprinkles and Pure & Simple are equally effective. This stitch can also be used for articles of clothing and borders. It is effective in one color, but is stunning in a combination of two threads in the same color or two color values of the same thread.

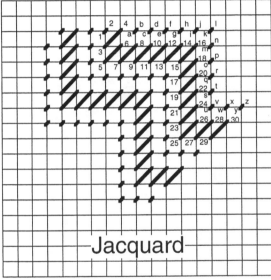

Jacquard

JERUSALEM CROSS (Rice Stitch Variation): This stitch is good for clothing, baskets, trees, and bushes. Try using a stranded cotton or silk for clothing and a matte cotton, Matte 18, or Rainbow Linen for baskets. Any of the overdyed threads, Sprinkles, or pearl cotton work well for trees and bushes.

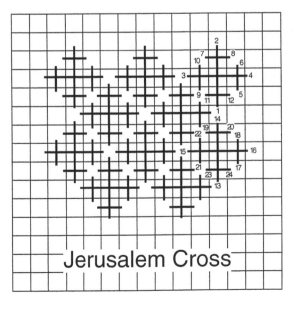

Jerusalem Cross

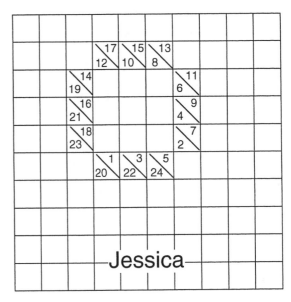

Jessica

JESSICA: This is one of the few stitches that creates a circle, and therefore is perfect for Christmas tree ornaments, flowers, and large buttons. Use a twisted thread such as one of the Kreinik Braids, Tiara, pearl cotton, or Trebizond for the best effect. Attach beads in the center of the stitch for a finishing touch.

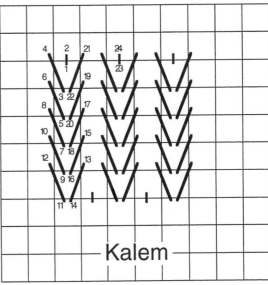

Kalem

KALEM (Knitting): This stitch can be used both vertically and horizontally. When stitched, it looks like it was knitted. Use it for sweaters, mittens, scarves, caps, and any other article of clothing you want to look "knitted". To create the most natural effect, stitch with a wool thread such as Medici, Persian wool, EPiC, Designer's Dream, or Appleton Crewel. Use Backgrounds Silk and Cream, Silk/Wool, or Impressions for a sweater with the elegance of cashmere!

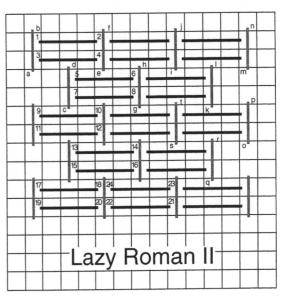

Lazy Roman II

LAZY ROMAN II: This stitch creates a woven effect and is ideal for a basket and Santa's bag. Try a textured thread such as Rainbow Linen or Per"Suede" for baskets. Use a softer thread such as wool or matte cotton for Santa's bag. Any overdyed thread will also create a wonderful effect with this stitch. If you are using a multi-ply overdyed thread, try reversing the plies in your needle for a mottled or tweeded effect. Also use this stitch for wicker furniture, paths, and rustic houses or log cabins.

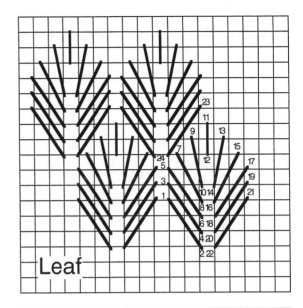

Leaf

LEAF: This is another stitch that is very good for trees, Christmas trees, bushes, and wreaths. One of the most effective ways to stitch this is with an overdyed thread such as Watercolours, Wildflowers, Waterlilies, Floss Overdyed, French Wool Overdyed, Pearl 8 Overdyed, Overture, Encore! or Bravo. This stitch can be used as a single motif (one leaf) or in a cluster.

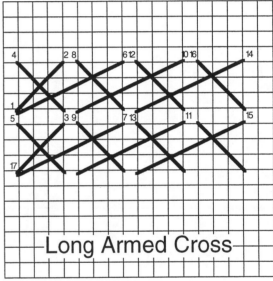

Long Armed Cross

LONG ARMED CROSS (Long-legged Cross, Portuguese, Plaited Slav): If stitched with one of the Kreinik Braids or Tiara, it looks like decorative braid, perfect for epaulets on nutcrackers and soldiers. This stitch creates braided Santa's bag handles, reindeer reins, horse reins, dog leashes, fence posts, and twisted looking fences. It is also effective when used with flat threads such as Neon Rays, Ribbon Floss, Fyre Werks, or one of the Kreinik Ribbons. This stitch can be done both horizontally and vertically, so it works in many places. It is also very effective as a border on clothing or a decorative dividing border on a Christmas stocking.

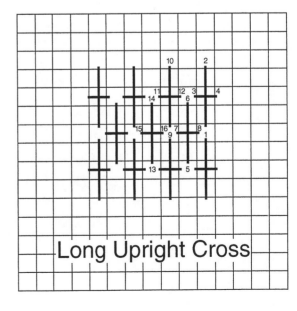

Long Upright Cross

LONG UPRIGHT CROSS: This stitch creates a woven-like effect that works well for a basket or Santa's bag. Try Rainbow Linen for a basket and Pure & Simple, French Wool Overdyed, Broider Wul, Medici, or pearl cotton for Santa's bag. This is also a very good background stitch that adds texture to your piece.

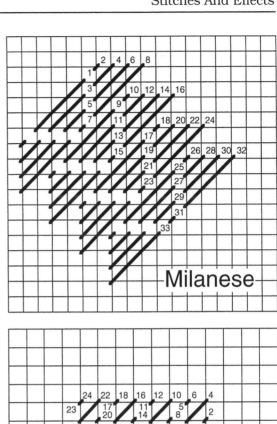

Milanese

MILANESE: You can create realistic mountains with this stitch by using Pebbly Perle, matte cotton, Matte 18 or an overdyed thread. It is also wonderful for Southwestern motifs, especially in an overdyed thread that combines the colors in your piece. This is an excellent background stitch. Your thread choice determines the look. Wool provides a soft and subtle effect while shiny threads such as pearl cotton, Floche, or silk are more vibrant.

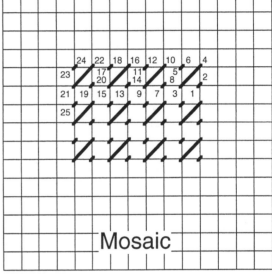

Mosaic

MOSAIC (Diagonal Hungarian Stitch): Like the Diagonal Mosaic, this is another very versatile stitch. It fits well into small areas and is easy to compensate. It creates outstanding architectural details such as window molding and frames, door frames and decorative accents. Consider the overdyed threads for these areas as well as Pebbly Perle, matte cotton, or Matte 18. Use pearl cotton and Floche to make these areas shine. This stitch is also good for clothing details such as cuffs and collars, and for larger articles of clothing such as dresses, pinafores, and coats. Decide on the look you want for the clothing, shiny or matte, before you choose the thread. If you choose an overdyed thread, try reversing some of the plies in your needle to give a mottled or tweeded effect. This is also an excellent background stitch.

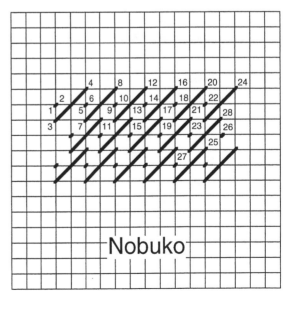

Nobuko

NOBUKO: The woven result created by this stitch is very effective in many places such as fish, water, mountains, trees, and sky as well as gingerbread houses, stucco houses and large areas of woodwork. It provides great texture for meadows, lawns, and snow covered areas. Try this stitch in any of the overdyed threads for water and sky. When using one of the overdyed threads, try reversing some of the plies or strands in your needle to create a mottled or tweeded effect. Fish are great in shiny thread such as pearl cotton, Patina, or Trebizond. Try matte cotton or Matte 18 for gingerbread or stucco houses. Use subtle shades of overdyed thread for woodwork. Try Flair or Rachel for snowy areas. This is also a wonderful background stitch and a great stitch with which to experiment.

NORWICH (Waffle): This is a great stitch for adding texture to square areas like quilts and Christmas packages. It also adds dimension to door panels, boxes, planters, and is even great for a jack-in-the-box. Christmas packages are most realistic when stitched with a metallic thread such as Kreinik Braid or Ribbon, Tiara, Candlelight or Gold Rush 18; or shiny threads such as Neon Rays or Ribbon Floss. Door panels are effective worked in matte cotton or Matte 18 and try pearl cotton, stranded cotton or any metallic thread for a jack-in-the-box. Consider stranded cotton or silk for quilt squares.

OBLIQUE SLAV: This slanted stitch gives wonderful texture to horizontal straight lines. It is perfect for wall or ceiling molding, decorative bands on clothing, and even fences. This is very effective stitched with one of the ribbon threads such as Neon Rays or Ribbon Floss. It also works well with a stranded cotton or silk such as Soie Cristale, Splendor, or Kreinik Silk Mori; however, you may need to increase the number of plies to get good canvas coverage.

OBLONG CROSS: The thread choice really dictates the look of this stitch. Worked in the finer sizes of pearl cotton, Wildflowers, Bravo! or Floche it appears almost lacy. In a thicker thread such as wool, Matte 18, or matte cotton it covers the canvas better and looks heavier. The stitch length can also be varied (1 row over 2 threads, alternating with 1 row over 3 threads high) which completely changes its appearance. Consider this stitch for jackets, pants, dresses and boots. This is also a wonderful background stitch.

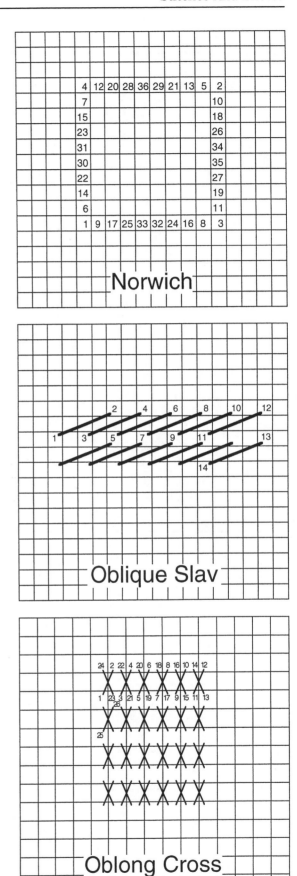

Norwich

Oblique Slav

Oblong Cross

OCTAGONAL RHODES: This is one of the few stitches that creates a circle and therefore can be very versatile. Think of this stitch for Christmas tree ornaments, balloons, holly berries, pompoms, bow centers, door knobs and other circular areas. It is quite effective stitched in twisted threads such as Kreinik Fine (#8) or Medium (#16) Braid, Tiara, Pizzaz, and Sprinkles, and in flat threads such as Neon Rays, Fyre Werks, or one of the Kreinik Ribbons. It is also effective in any of the overdyed threads or the combination threads such as Rachelette or Frosty Rays.

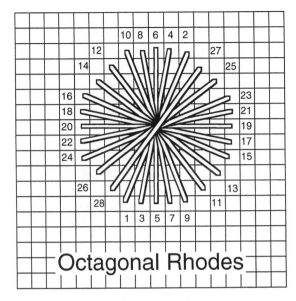

Octagonal Rhodes

OLD FLORENTINE (OldParisian): This bargello variation is very effective for roofs, roads, paths, and chimneys. Stranded threads are most effective in this stitch because they spread. Be sure to lay them carefully so that they lay flat on your canvas. Watercolours, Encore!, French Wool Overdyed, Floss Overdyed, Bravo, and Wildflowers are all very effective in this stitch. Consider this stitch in Rachel or Flair for snow on rooftops; it shimmers and gives texture at the same time. This is also an excellent background stitch.

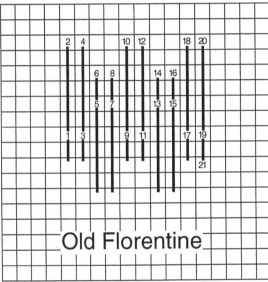

Old Florentine

ORIENTAL: This is a great stitch for sky and water, especially in one of the overdyed threads. It is also effective in a shiny thread such as Neon Rays, Ribbon Floss, Floche, Trebizond or Kreinik Silk Serica. It is a wonderful background stitch in almost every thread.

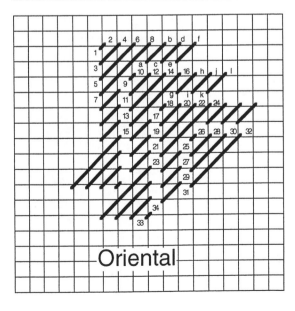

Oriental

OVERLAID OBLONG CROSS: This is a wonderful clothing stitch. Think of it for jackets, coats, pants or even hats. You can use the same thread for both layers or combine two threads of the same color such as pearl cotton and Patina, Floche and Wildflowers or Bravo, Sprinkles and Pure & Simple, or Neon Rays and Tiara. You can also combine these threads in two different colors for a unique look.

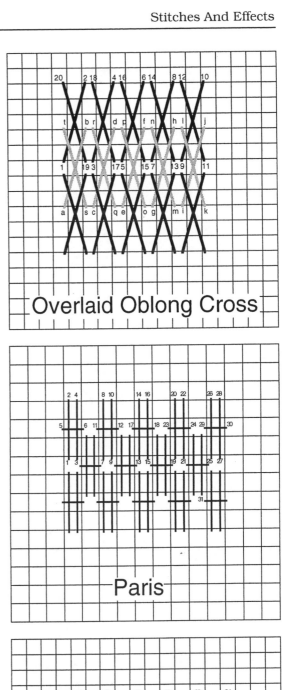

PARIS (Double and Tie Stitch): This stitch creates a very textured look in clothing. It almost looks like brocade when stitched with Trebizond. If you are using 13 or 14 mesh canvas, try stitching with #5 pearl cotton. It does not look as heavy. This is also effective in metallic threads such as one of the Kreinik Braids, Tiara, or Candlelight. Floche is also very effective when used in this stitch; try 2 strands on 18 mesh and 3/4 strands on 13/14 mesh canvas. The woven effect created is good for baskets, tree trunks, flowers, animals, and sea shells. This is a good background stitch and a place where two threads could be alternated.

PARISIAN: This is a small stitch that is easy to compensate and works well in small areas. It is especially effective for animals, fish, bird feathers, sky, water, and even clothing. Try wool, Rainbow Linen, matte cotton, Matte 18, Floche or stranded silk for animals. Any of the overdyed threads are very effective for sky and water. This is a good place to try reversing some of the plies in your needle to create a mottled or tweeded effect. Try pearl cotton, matte cotton, stranded cotton or silk, or wool for clothing. This is an excellent background stitch for both small and large pieces.

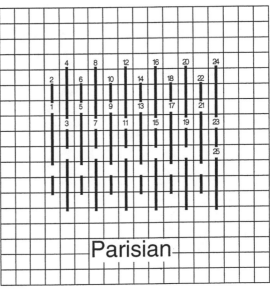

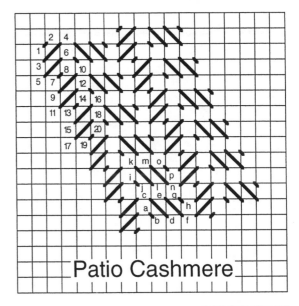

Patio Cashmere

PATIO CASHMERE: This is an architectural stitch for patios, walls, houses, and roofs, and also works well for paths, roads, and mountains. Your thread choice is limitless and dependent upon the look you want to create. Rainbow Linen creates a textured path or patio and pearl or matte cotton creates a smooth look for those areas. To produce a shaded effect, try using a monochromatic overdyed thread.

PAVILLION BOXES: This is an excellent clothing stitch when worked in stranded cotton or wool such as EPiC. Impressions, stranded silk, or matte cotton also work well in this stitch. Use a thinner thread for the diagonal lines. If you're using #5 pearl cotton for the diamond shapes, then use #8 or #12 pearl cotton for the diagonal lines. Consider using a metallic such as Kreinik Very Fine (#4) or Fine (#8) Braid, Candlelight, Pizzaz, Sprinkles or Tiara for the diagonal lines to really add dimension to the piece. Any of the overdyed threads are very effective in the diamond shapes of this stitch along with a solid pearl cotton, stranded cotton or silk for the diagonal lines.

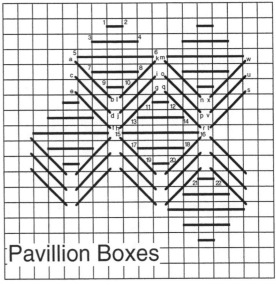

Pavillion Boxes

PAVILLION DIAMONDS (2-4-6-4-2 Stitch, Hungarian Diamond): This stitch is very effective for clothing. Consider it for long Santa coats using Spring II, Kreinik Silk Serica, EPiC, Broider Wul, Twedie 18, French Wool Overdyed, Medici, Paternayan or Silk/Wool. Reverse the stitch direction of the sleeves in clothing to give more definition to the piece. Also use this stitch to create a wallpaper pattern with two colors or two very close color values. This is also a very good background stitch.

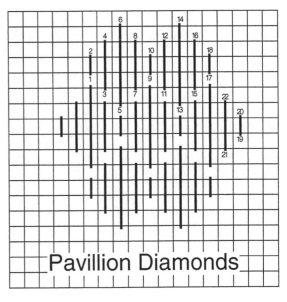

Pavillion Diamonds

POINT DE TRESSE: This stitch creates a plaited effect that is good for columns or borders. The thread choice is unlimited. One of the overdyed threads is especially effective for a column. For a border, choose a thread that contrasts with the other threads in your design. If the rest of the piece is stitched in wool, then try pearl cotton, matte cotton or a silk for the border, but use one of the colors within the design.

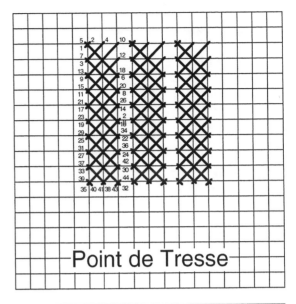

Point de Tresse

RECTANGULAR RHODES: This is an ideal stitch for belt and shoe buckles, especially when stitched with a metallic such as Kreinik Braid, Tiara, Pizzaz, Sprinkles, or Candlelight. It fits into rectangular spaces to add texture and can also be repeated to create a very distinctive border. This stitch is more effective worked in braids, or twisted threads such as pearl cotton, Trebizond, Pebbly Perle, Watercolours, Overture or Wildflowers because the stitch elements show more distinctly.

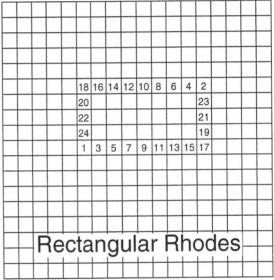

Rectangular Rhodes

REVERSE SCOTCH: This stitch creates a wonderful checkerboard effect that works well for houses, inner door shadowing, and inside window shadowing. Use this stitch for blankets, quilts, clothing, or any checkered motif. For architectural detailing, try a monochromatic multicolored thread to eliminate the need to shade. This stitch is most effective when worked in a stranded cotton or silk or even try stripping Pebbly Perle for a matte look. Lightly twisted threads such as pearl cotton, Watercolours, Encore!, Overture, and matte cotton or Matte 18 also work very well. This is also a wonderful background stitch in which you could change colors or even threads for the alternating stitches.

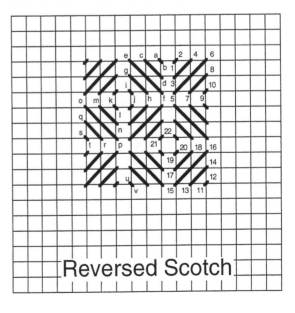

Reversed Scotch

RHODES: This is a great stitch to use to add texture to a piece. It also adds dimension to door panels, boxes, planters, Christmas packages, or any square area. Christmas packages are most realistic when stitched with a metallic thread such as Kreinik Braid or Ribbon, Tiara, Candlelight, Gold Rush 18, or shiny threads such as Neon Rays or Ribbon Floss. Door panels are effective in matte cotton or Matte 18. Make a thread choice based on the effect you wish to achieve: shiny, matte, or multi-colored. Single strand and multi-plied threads are equally effective in this stitch.

RHODES HEART: This stitch adds decorative texture to heart shaped areas. It can be enlarged to fit any space. Floche, stranded cotton, Soie Cristale, Splendor, Soie d'Alger, and Kreinik Silk Mori are very effective in this stitch. Be sure to lay the threads carefully. Tightly twisted threads such as Trebizond and Patina are not as effective since they do not cover the canvas as well. Other good choices are Flair, Frosty Rays, Rachel, Rachelette, Neon Rays, Ribbon Floss, matte cotton, wool, and the overdyed threads.

RICE: (William & Mary, Crossed Corners): This stitch creates great decorative borders, especially when worked in two different colors or two different threads. For example, in the first row stitch the cross in one color or thread and the corner tie downs in another color or thread. In the next row reverse the colors or threads. Consider using one thread for the large cross and a different thread or color for the corner tie downs throughout the design. The thread choice is unlimited. A metallic such as Kreinik Braid, Tiara, Candlelight, Sprinkles, or Gold Rush 18 is especially effective in this stitch. With an overdyed thread, matte cotton, Matte 18, or Pebbly Perle, this stitch creates decorative bricks for a house or a wall. Also try this stitch for snow-covered bushes using an overdyed thread for the large cross and a white metallic or Snow for the corner tie downs.

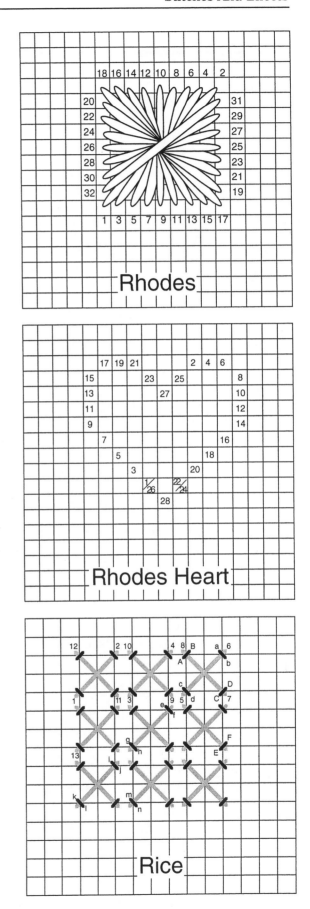

Rhodes

Rhodes Heart

Rice

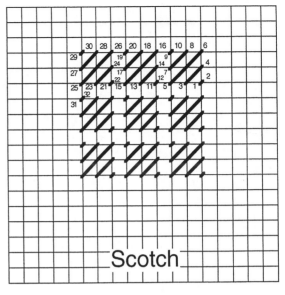

SCOTCH (Flat Stitch, Diagonal Satin Stitch): This is a very versatile stitch that can be used in any square area in your design. It is effective for houses, especially to add texture to large plain areas such as walls, paths, and roads. It works well for door and window molding, clothing and backgrounds. Almost any thread you choose should work very well in this stitch.

Scotch

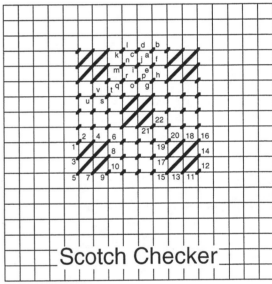

SCOTCH CHECKER (Chequer): The use of any colored thread for the Scotch element and white thread for the basketweave portion creates the look of gingham fabric. This is especially good for children's clothing and kitchen decorations. To add texture to clothing, walls, sky, and fields use the same color for both elements of the stitch. Floche, stranded cotton or silk, pearl cotton, matte cotton, wool, Neon Rays and Ribbon Floss are very effective in this stitch. This is an excellent background stitch.

Scotch Checker

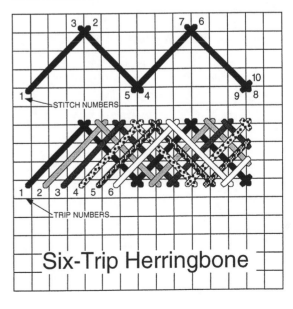

SIX-TRIP HERRINGBONE: This stitch creates magnificent house clapboards when stitched with an overdyed thread such as Watercolours or Overture. It is also extremely effective as a border, especially using 3 different colors of thread. Try one of the Kreinik Braids, Candlelight, or Tiara for glitter and Neon Rays or Ribbon Floss for shine. Twisted threads work as well as flat threads. You may even want to combine 2 or 3 different threads. This stitch is not easy to compensate, so be sure you have enough canvas threads for the pattern.

Six-Trip Herringbone

SLANTED GOBELIN: The slanted variation of the Gobelin is as versatile as its straight counterpart. Try using it in those small areas where you want a smoother look than tent stitching will give. This stitch will give definition to shapes and will move more quickly than tent stitching. It can cover 2, 3, or more threads depending on your needs. The Slanted Gobelin is quite effective in threads like stranded cotton or silk, Floche, Medici, Broider Wul, or Appleton Crewel. It is also very effective stitched in Ribbon Floss or Neon Rays (be sure to lay it carefully). Pearl cotton, matte cotton, Matte 18, Pebbly Perle, Pure & Simple, and Sprinkles also work very well. This is the ideal stitch for Per"Suede" and Ultra Suede. Just be sure that it lays flat on the back of the canvas as well as on the front.

SMYRNA CROSS (Double Cross): Try this stitch for stars, flowers, lacy dresses, and even as molding on gingerbread houses. It is most effective when worked with a fine, twisted or braided thread that shows all the stitch elements. Try Snow, Kreinik Braid, Tiara, Antica or Candlelight for stars. Use pearl cotton, Trebizond, Patina, Wildflowers, stranded cotton or silk for flowers and dresses. When using pearl cotton, you may want to try the finer sizes to really show off the stitch.

SPLIT ENCROACHING GOBELIN: This stitch is very effective for adding snow to rooftops, grass on lawns, and creating mountainsides. Stranded cotton or silk, Medici, Broider Wul, Appleton Crewel, Designer's Dream or Paternayan work best in this stitch. They are easier to lay side by side which results in an even look. Try combining wool and a fine metallic braid or blending filament for snow that glistens.

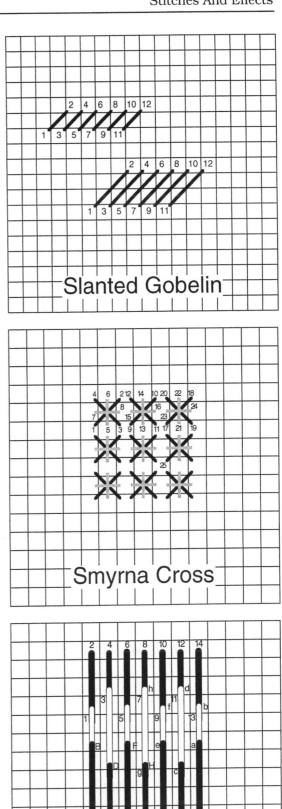

Slanted Gobelin

Smyrna Cross

Split Encroaching Gobelin

SPRATS HEAD: This stitch creates the perfect triangle for those triangular-shaped areas of your design. It works in border spaces, in clothing openings, and as a decorative accent over a door or a window. Floche, stranded cotton or silk, Medici, Broider Wul, and Appleton Crewel and wide threads such as Flair, Rachel, Neon Rays and Ribbon Floss work very well for this stitch. Be sure to lay the threads carefully so the stitch looks smooth and flat.

Sprats Head

SPRATS HEAD HEART: A variation of the basic Sprats Head, this stitch creates a stunning textured heart. Consider it for decorative borders or filling in any heart-shaped space. This is another place for stranded cotton and silk or wide, flat threads such as Flair, Rachel, Neon Rays, or Kreinik Ribbon.

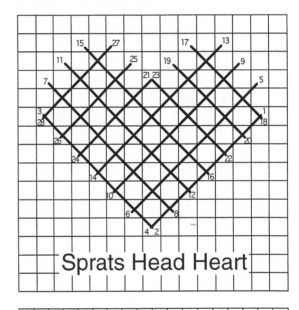

Sprats Head Heart

SQUARE EYELET (Algerian Eye): Stitched in a cluster, this creates a lacy look for ruffles, pinafores or dresses. You may stitch over any even number of threads, whichever best suits your piece. Try varying the size within an area for the look of patterned lace. Use pearl cotton, Floche or stranded cotton for ruffles and try Patina or Trebizond for areas you want to shine.

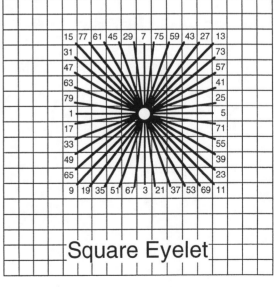

Square Eyelet

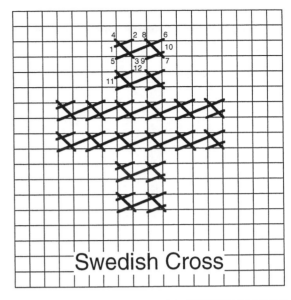

Swedish Cross

SWEDISH CROSS: This unique stitch creates wonderful textured crosses. It is not easy to compensate, so only try this in large areas. The length and width of the cross can be varied to fit your piece, and the vertical bar can be longer than the horizontal bar. Any of the metallic threads like Kreinik Braid, Tiara, Candlelight, and Gold Rush 18; or shiny threads such as Trebizond, pearl cotton, Neon Rays, Ribbon Floss, or Kreinik Silk Serica are very effective in this stitch.

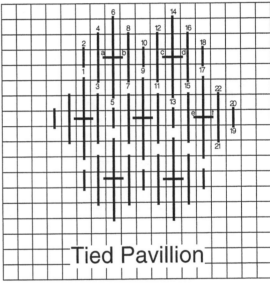

Tied Pavillion

TIED PAVILLION: This is a very effective clothing stitch, especially if the tie down is worked in a metallic thread such as Kreinik Braid, Kreinik Cord, Pizzaz, Tiara, or Candlelight. The basic pavillion can be stitched in almost any thread; however, a stranded thread provides better coverage. Choose a thread to suit the look desired for your design area: shiny, matte, metallic, or multi-colored. This is also an excellent background stitch, either in a one-thread or in a two-thread combination.

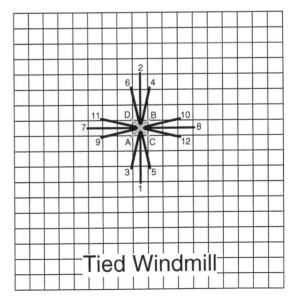

Tied Windmill

TIED WINDMILL: This is an excellent stitch for flowers as it gives good texture and dimension. Try using pearl cotton, Floche, Trebizond, or Soie Cristale for a shiny look or an overdyed thread for a multi-colored look. To create a decorative accent on clothing try using a contrasting thread color or type for definition. This will also be very effective for stars. Try using Snow, Tiara, or Kreinik Braid.

TURKEY WORK (Turkey Knot Stitch, Turkey Knot Tufting): This stitch, when cut, looks like fur and is ideal for a beard, hair, fur coats, fur trim, curly haired animals, wreaths, and garlands. On 18 mesh canvas use 2 or 3 strands of fine wool such as Medici, Designer's Dream, Broider Wul or Appleton Crewel for a fuller and thicker look. On 13/14 mesh canvas use 4 or 5 strands of fine wool or 1 or 2 strands of Persian wool. Try using French Wool Overdyed for a shaded effect. You may cut the thread after you have finished stitching for a furrier effect or leave the loops uncut for a curlier effect. This stitch should be worked from the bottom up.

UPRIGHT CROSS (Straight Cross): This stitch fits well in small areas and gives great texture to your piece. In clothing, it creates a textured look that is most effective in twisted, shiny threads such as Patina, Trebizond, and pearl cotton. If Turkey Work and French Knots are not your favorites, consider this stitch for fur trim on clothing and Santa's suit. If you use a finer metallic braid than usual for your canvas size, this stitch creates a rough, glittery effect. It is also effective with stranded cotton or silk, and wool.

UPRIGHT ORIENTAL: This unique stitch gives the effect of movement and is therefore great for water and sky. Try using two threads of the same color: one for the 2-4-6 row and another for the 3-3-3 row. Consider using two different colors or two close values of the same color. Some good thread combinations are Impressions and Rachel, metallic ribbon and Flair, pearl cotton and wool, and stranded cotton or silk with an overdyed thread. This is an excellent background stitch and gives light coverage if you choose a fine metallic such as Kreinik Very Fine (#4) or Fine (#8) Braid, Tiara, Snow, or Candlelight. Use a stranded cotton or silk, or wool for heavier coverage. A wonderful effect can be achieved with the use of either light or dark colors.

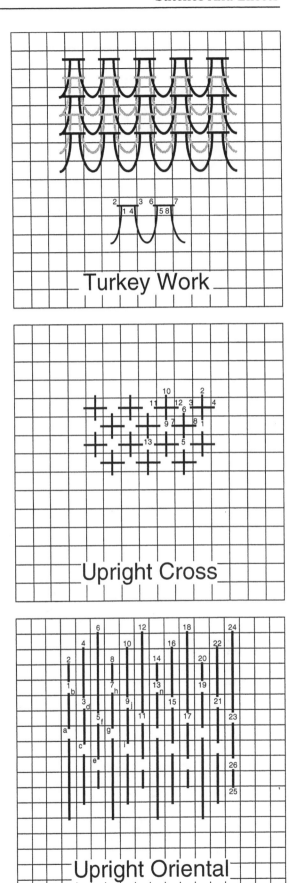

Turkey Work

Upright Cross

Upright Oriental

VAN DYKE: The braided effect created by this stitch is perfect for carpets and area rugs, especially for rag rugs. This is also an excellent stitch for doll house rugs. Try using Floss Overdyed, Madras, French Wool Overdyed, EPiC, Watercolours, Overture, Bravo, or Wildflowers for a multi-colored effect. This stitch can be worked either vertically or horizontally. Worked in wool or Impressions, it gives a knitted look to sweaters, mittens or any other article of clothing. When using this stitch, end your thread at the bottom of each row then start back at the top for the next row.

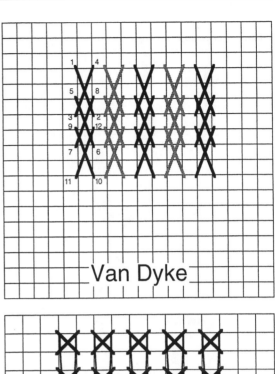

Van Dyke

VELVET: This stitch creates a fuzzy effect that is excellent for hair, beards, and fur on coats. Use Wisper or Kit Kin for a light wispy effect. Try using wool, Santa's Beard and Suit, or Alpaca 18 for a heavy, furrier effect. These loops are not cut, so it is important to keep their length consistent for an even look. This stitch should be worked from the bottom up.

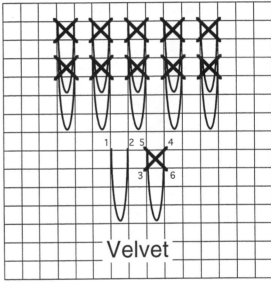

Velvet

VICTORIAN STEP: This is a marvelous clothing stitch, especially for long coats, capes or dresses. Try 2 or 3 close values of stranded cotton or silk for a truly stunning effect. The use of two complementing threads such as Soie Cristale with Impressions, stranded cotton or Floche with a metallic braid, or Waterlilies with Soie Cristale or stranded cotton, creates a wonderful effect. These thread combinations also produce a very distinctive background.

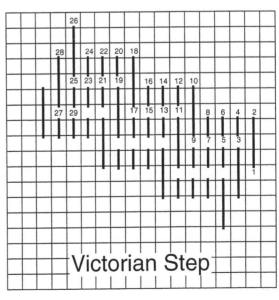

Victorian Step

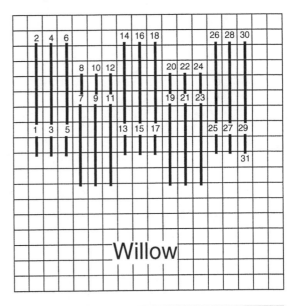

WHEAT STITCH (Sheaf Stitch, Shell Stitch): This stitch can be worked over four or six vertical threads to fit the area you wish to cover. This is a striking decorative accent for gardens, fields, or any other landscape area. It is especially effective when stitched with stranded threads such as stranded cotton or silk, Floche, or with any of the overdyed threads. This is also a great accent stitch for Halloween canvases.

WILLOW: This bargello variation is excellent for shingles, roofs, houses, or baskets. It is wonderful when stitched with threads such as Paternayan, Appleton Crewel, Medici, Designer's Dream, stranded cotton or silk, or Floche. Wider, flat threads such as Rachel, Rachelette, Flair, or Frosty Rays are also very effective in this stitch. This is an excellent background stitch for large areas.

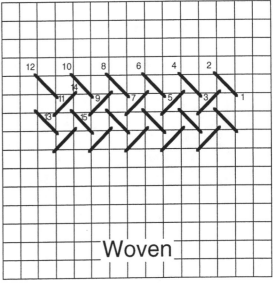

WOVEN (Web): This stitch creates a textured look that works well in Santa's bag, baskets, grass, and tree tops. Try using pearl cotton, Pure & Simple, wool, or Rainbow Linen for Santa's bag or for a basket. An overdyed thread such as Wildflowers, Watercolours, Pearl 8 Overdyed, Overture, Encore!, or Bravo! works well for grass and trees.

WOVEN SPIDER: This stitch creates wonderful round Christmas tree ornaments, flowers, hair buns, round candies and wheels. It is especially effective with stranded cotton or silk, Sprinkles, Candlelight, Kreinik Braid, or Tiara. Try using wool or French Wool Overdyed for hair. To work the woven spider web, move your needle over and then under the laid spokes.

To create a different effect, lay your foundation with an even number of spokes (usually 6). When working this stitch, referred to as a Smooth Spider Web, bring your needle up close to one of the laid spokes. Then, working on top of the canvas or fabric, move your needle over 2 spokes and then go back under 1 spoke. The under spoke is always the second spoke your needle has just passed over.

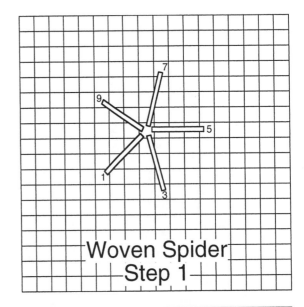

Woven Spider
Step 1

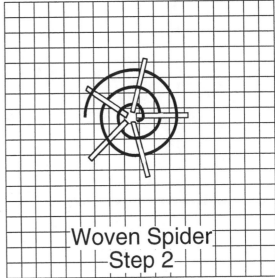

Woven Spider
Step 2

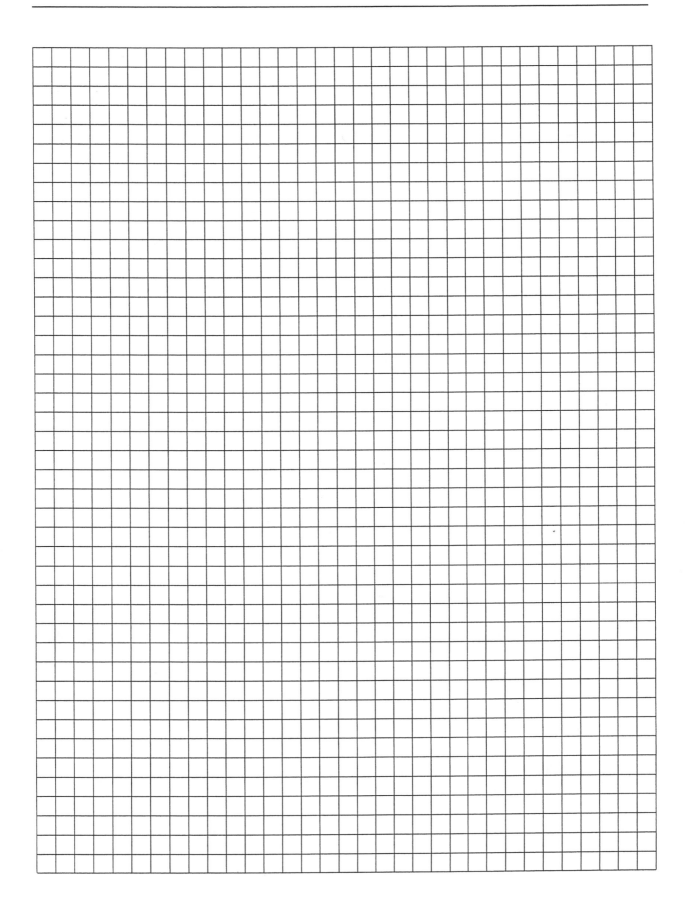

BIBLIOGRAPHY

Alderson, Chottie. **Stitch Fair**. Banning, CA: Self-published.

Ambuter, Carolyn. **Carolyn Ambuter's Even More Complete Book Of Needlepoint**. New York: Harper & Row, Publishers, 1972.

Caswell, Ann. **Fibers, Threads, Yarns, & Other Embellishments Section I**. Reston, VA: Self-published. 1991.

Caswell, Ann. **Fibers, Threads, Yarns, & Other Embellishments Section II**. Reston, VA: Self-published. 1991.

Caswell, Ann. **Thread Update**. Reston, VA: Self-published. 1995.

Christensen, Jo Ippolito. **The Needlepoint Book**. Englewood Cliffs, NJ: Prentice Hall Press. 1976.

"Decorative Threads." **Needle Pointers**. April/May 1990, p.44.

Dulle, Sue. **Diagonal Darning**. Kansas City, MO: Self-published. 1990.

Golden Gate Canvas Workers Chapter. **A Background Stitch Reference Book Revised Edition**. Belmont, CA: Self-published. 1988.

Hilton, Jean. **Jean Hilton's Needlepoint Stitches**. Westminster, CA: Self-published. 1989.

Hilton, Jean. **Jean Hilton's Stimulating Stitches**. Flint, MI: Self-published, 1992.

Pearson, Anna. **Needlepoint Stitch By Stitch**. New York: Ballantine Books. 1987.

Pearson, Anna. **The Complete Needlepoint Course**. Radnor, PA: Chilton Book Co. 1991.

Rhodes, Mary. **Dictionary Of Canvas Work Stitches**. New York: Charles Scribner's Sons. 1980.

Simon, Sally. **Darned Easy**. Southfield MI: Self-published, 1981.

Taggart, Jean. **Laid Fillings For Evenweave Fabrics**. Houston, TX: Brockton Publishing Co. 1995.

The Royal School of Needlework Book of Needlework and Embroidery. Edited by Lanto Synge. London: Wm. Collins Sons & Co. Ltd. 1986.

"Watercolours." **Needle Pointers**, April/May 1991, pp.4-6.

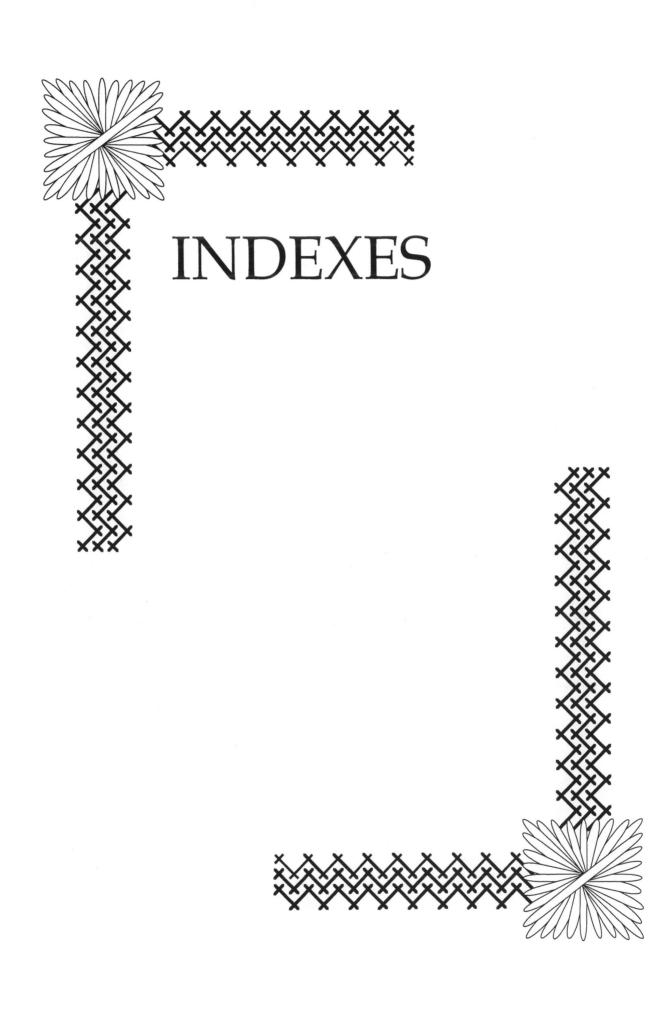

INDEXES

THREAD INDEX

Stitches For Effect

W

Watercolours · 3, 7, 11, 12, 13, 19, 20, 22, 23, 24, 27, 29, 30, 32, 35, 36, 39, 42, 45, 47, 52, 53, 55
Waterlilies · 11, 12, 13, 19, 20, 23, 29, 30, 31, 37, 39, 52
Wildflowers · 7, 8, 11, 12, 13, 19, 20, 22, 23, 24, 27, 28, 29, 30, 32, 36, 39, 41, 42, 43, 45, 48, 52, 53
Wisper · 16, 19, 21, 26, 32, 35, 52
Wool · 2, 7, 11, 12, 14, 15, 16, 22, 23, 24, 26, 27, 29, 30, 31, 32, 33, 35, 37, 38, 40, 41, 43, 44, 45, 46, 47, 48, 51, 52, 53, 54

STITCH INDEX

EFFECT INDEX

A

GENERAL INDEX